Don't Feel Guilty, Eat It!

By: Luis Bruno
Photography by: Joe Lee
Edited by: Kathleen Bruno

To: MAMIE,

COOK FROM THE
HEART!

Eclectic
Publishing

I dedicate this book with love, "two worlds' worth,"

to my beautiful wife, Kathleen, and amazing daughter, Emma,

both of whom I admire and adore.

Copyright© 2008 Eclectic Publishing
ISBN 978-0-9821182-0-7 0-9821182-0-1 Hardcover
ISBN 978-0-9821182-1-4 0-9821182-1-X Softcover
Printed in USA
Photography by Joe Lee Photography
Edited by Kathleen Bruno

www.brunoseclectic.com

Contents

Acknowledgments

Special thanks are due to the many friends who have helped me and worked so hard to get this book pulled together, but first I want to say thanks to Mississippi. If my wife hadn't brought me from New York to her home state, I don't know where I would be. The warm and wonderful people of this great state have truly saved me. Thank You!

Kathleen, thank you for your incredible palate and amazing knowledge of food. I could not have done this book without you. We make a pretty good team, don't we? Thanks for being there for me - and for making sure we did it right!

Thank you to both of my mothers for believing in me and for keeping me on that straight line. Love you Irma and Martha!

Next I would like to thank Joe Lee for the remarkable food photography in this book. Wow! Hats off to you, and thanks for all your hard work. You really are an amazing artist. Can't wait until… the next one?

To Liza Looser and *The Cirlot Agency*, I am forever grateful for your inspired ideas and endless creativity in designing the book layout and super hot cover. It is easy to see why you guys are the best! Thank you for believing in me.

Matt Huffman, Shannon Smith and Dowden Morrow - if it weren't for you three, I never would have finished testing the recipes. Many thanks for being such great friends and for making sure the recipes were accurate, easy to follow and delicious!

To *Persnickety* and *Top It Off*, thank you for being top-notch professionals. Your generosity and graciousness in allowing me unlimited access to your beautiful dishes and tabletop lines are appreciated more than you know. It certainly made Joe's artistic food photography even more special.

Thank you *Antonelli College* for having such talented students and an impressive graphic design program. Ashley Bieliauskas, Instructor at Antonelli College and owner of Scratch Design™, and students Shaina Boblick and Rebekah Burris, big thanks to you for all the time and energy you have put into the layout of this book.

Pearl River Glassware, thanks for the exquisite Bruno's Eclectic Glassware that you developed - and for trusting me to take this adventure with you.

Bill and Sara Ray - what can I say but THANK YOU from the bottom of my heart - for being such great friends, foodies and for always believing in me.

Introduction

How do you become a 400-pound man? It's really not that hard when your whole life has pretty much been defined by your relationship with food. For most of my years, this relationship has been unhealthy and addictive and at one point-life threatening. I was forced to make dramatic changes in my eating habits and lifestyle, and as a result, I have turned my life around. The purpose of this cookbook is to share with you some things I have learned through this journey that can make eating healthy fun and delicious.

Born and raised in the Bronx, NY, I weighed in at a whopping two pounds and have been making up for that low weight ever since! My early years were very difficult having to experience life on welfare in a home with no father figure surrounded by alcoholism and drug abuse; suffer the loss of five family members in a two year period; and live with a sense of hopelessness as far as educational and career opportunities. I left home at age 13 to live with my brother in upstate New York and work for him at the family deli. He paid me with food, and by the time I was 17, I weighed 275 pounds!

Realizing that I needed to escape this life of excess stress and food, I made the decision to move to Florida and attend culinary school. However, within 18 months, I had gained an additional 125 pounds.

I met, fell in love with and married my wife Kathleen during this time, and we eventually moved to her hometown of Jackson, Mississippi. Our love of food and cooking created a comfort zone of eating, no exercise and the beginning stages of diabetes for me. We realized our dream of opening a restaurant, but with that dream came enormous stress and the availability of meals such as rib eye sandwiches for breakfast, caramel custard for dinner and a six-pack before bed. My wake up call came when I was taking 6 shots of insulin a day, suffering reflux, cirrhosis of the liver, blurred vision and the loss of feeling in my right foot. The doctor gave me very little hope if I continued at this rate. I was put on an extreme, medically-monitored liquid diet of only 800 calories a day. With the motivation of living to see my little daughter Emma grow up, I lost 160 pounds in 5½ months and an additional 40 pounds after that by eating healthy and exercising.

I know my story is extreme, but I wanted to share it with you so that you will understand where I am coming from. This is not a diet book—this is a way to give yourself permission to eat and enjoy without guilt. That's what I'm talkin' about! Invite some friends over, share some crab fritters and a mango martini. Savor the moment and relish the memory!

In Loving Memory
of
Brenda Cothren Smith

Starters

Chicken Satay

Makes 2 dozen skewers

4 (6-ounce)	boneless, skinless chicken breasts
3 tablespoons	oyster sauce*
½ (13.5-ounce) can	unsweetened coconut milk* (or light coconut milk)
2 tablespoons	granulated sugar (or Splenda®)
¼ cup	canola oil
1 tablespoon	curry powder
1½ teaspoons	ground turmeric
	Thai Peanut Sauce (recipe follows), as an accompaniment
	Thai Cucumber Salad (recipe follows), as an accompaniment

1. Cut each breast lengthwise into 6 slices. In a large bowl, whisk together the oyster sauce, coconut milk, sugar, oil, curry powder and tumeric. Reserve ½ cup sauce for basting the chicken while grilling. Marinate the chicken in the remaining sauce for at least 4 hours or up to overnight.

2. Thread the marinated chicken strips onto bamboo skewers which have been soaked in water for at least 30 minutes. Discard the marinade. Preheat the grill to medium-high; clean and oil the grates to prevent sticking. Grill the chicken until just cooked through, about 3 minutes on each side. Baste with the reserved sauce while grilling. Serve hot or at room temperature with Thai Peanut Sauce and Thai Cucumber Salad.

Thai Peanut Sauce
Makes 2 cups

1½ teaspoons	canola oil
1 teaspoon	Thai red curry paste,* or to taste
½ (13.5-ounce) can	unsweetened coconut milk* (or light coconut milk)
¼ cup	granulated sugar (or Splenda®)
½ teaspoon	kosher salt, or to taste
1 teaspoon	fish sauce* (preferably Squid brand)
1 teaspoon	Knorr® Tamarind Soup Base* (or juice of one lime)
½ cup	peanut butter
1 tablespoon	chopped roasted peanuts, for garnish

1. Heat the oil in a small saucepan over medium-high heat; add the curry paste, and stir occasionally until the aroma is released, about 1 to 2 minutes.

2. Add the coconut milk, sugar, salt, fish sauce and tamarind soup base (or lime juice). Bring to a boil. Taste and adjust the seasoning as needed.

3. Remove the pan from the heat, and whisk in the peanut butter. Transfer to a sauce bowl, and garnish with chopped peanuts.

Thai Cucumber Salad
Serves 6

1 cup	white vinegar
½ cup	granulated sugar (or Splenda®)
2 medium	English cucumbers, peeled
2 medium	shallots, peeled and finely sliced
1 medium	fresh jalapeño, cut into paper-thin slices
¼ teaspoon	kosher salt, or to taste

1. Combine the vinegar and sugar in a small saucepan; simmer over medium-high heat until the sugar completely dissolves and the mixture has reduced slightly, about 10 minutes. Set aside to cool.

2. Cut the cucumbers in half lengthwise, then thinly slice into half-rounds.

3. Add the cucumbers, shallots, jalapeños and salt to the cooled syrup, and mix thoroughly. Taste, and adjust the seasoning as needed with salt; serve chilled or at room temperature.

*Available at your local Asian market

Rellenos de Papa
(Stuffed Potato Balls)
Makes 15 potato balls

Filling:

3 tablespoons	extra-virgin olive oil, divided
1 pound	ground chuck (or ground turkey)
1 teaspoon	kosher salt, or to taste
2 tablespoons	Bruno's Dry Adobo Seasoning (or your favorite adobo), or to taste
½ medium	yellow onion, finely diced
1 (8-ounce) can	tomato sauce
2 tablespoons	small capers
¼ cup	fresh cilantro leaves, chopped

Potatoes:

3 pounds	russet potatoes, peeled and cut into eighths
1 large	egg
1 tablespoon	cornstarch, plus extra as needed
½ teaspoon	kosher salt, or to taste
½ teaspoon	Bruno's Dry Adobo Seasoning (or your favorite adobo), or to taste
	canola oil, for frying

For the Filling:

1. Place a large sauté pan over medium-high heat; add 2 tablespoons of the oil and heat through. Season the beef with the salt and adobo and cook until brown and cooked through, about 5 minutes; drain the beef in a colander, and set aside. Do not wipe out the pan.

2. Place the sauté pan back over medium heat; add the remaining oil and heat through. Cook the onions until tender, about 5 to 8 minutes.

3. Add the meat back to the pan along with the tomato sauce and capers; simmer until the mixture has reduced and thickened, about 15 to 20 minutes. Stir in the cilantro, then taste and adjust the seasoning as needed with salt and adobo. Remove from the heat, and set aside to cool completely.

4. Boil the potatoes in salted water until tender, about 30 minutes. Drain well, then pass through a ricer or mash with a potato masher.

5. Whisk together the egg, cornstarch, salt and adobo; stir into the mashed potatoes. (Do NOT over-mix the potatoes, or they will become gummy.) Taste, and adjust the seasoning as needed with salt and adobo. Allow the potato mixture to cool completely.

6. Divide the cooled potato mixture into 15 equal portions. Dust the palms of your hands with cornstarch, and spread the potato mixture in the palm of one hand. Spoon a small amount of filling into the center of the mixture, then enclose the filling with the potato mixture. Coat the stuffed potato ball lightly with cornstarch, and continue making balls in this manner until all of the ingredients have been used.

7. Heat the oil in a deep fryer or a large, deep saucepan to 360 degrees F. Fry the stuffed potato balls until golden brown; drain on paper towels briefly before serving.

Louie's Note: This is one of my favorite childhood foods – fried stuffed mashed potatoes! What could be better? Try serving these with Avocado-Lime Crema (see recipe on page 102).

Grilled Bread with Smoked Salmon, Manchego and Olives

Serves 4

2 cloves	garlic, peeled
1 to 2 pinches	kosher salt
3 tablespoons	extra-virgin olive oil
8 slices	French bread (or whole-grain French bread), ½-inch thick, cut at a sharp diagonal
2 medium	ripe red tomatoes, thinly sliced
⅛ teaspoon	freshly ground black pepper
8 ounces	cold-smoked salmon (or hot-smoked salmon)
½ cup	shaved manchego cheese (or Parmesan cheese) (2 ounces)
¼ cup	olive tapenade or relish (or chopped pitted olives), for garnish

1. Preheat the grill to medium. Clean and oil the grates to prevent sticking.

2. Mash the garlic and salt with a mortar and pestle (or the side of your chef's knife) to make a fine paste. Combine the garlic mixture and olive oil in a small bowl.

3. Grill the bread until golden brown, about 30 seconds to 1 minute per side.

4. Remove the bread from the grill; while still warm, lightly spread the garlic mixture on each slice. Top each with a tomato slice, and sprinkle with pepper. Place a 1-ounce slice of salmon over each tomato slice, then sprinkle about one tablespoonful of cheese over each. Garnish with tapenade, and serve warm or at room temperature.

Marinated Olives

Makes 2 (1-pint) jars of olives

4 cups	your favorite olives, pitted
2 teaspoons	crushed red pepper flakes, or to taste
1 tablespoon	chopped fresh rosemary
1 tablespoon	dried oregano
1 tablespoon	dried thyme
1 teaspoon	fennel seeds
1 tablespoon	whole black peppercorns
¼ teaspoon	kosher salt
6 medium	bay leaves
	zest of two lemons
	extra-virgin olive oil, as needed

1. Place the olives in a large bowl; add the crushed red pepper flakes, rosemary, oregano, thyme, fennel seeds, peppercorns, salt, bay leaves and lemon zest. Toss to combine.

2. Pack the olives in pint jars, making sure each jar has two bay leaves and that the ingredients are well distributed. Pour enough oil over the olives to cover, then tightly seal the jars.

3. Refrigerate for at least 4 days, shaking the jar a couple of times each day. (Store in the refrigerator for up to 2 weeks.)

Spicy Bacon–Wrapped Grilled Shrimp

Serves 4

20 jumbo	shrimp (about 1 pound - 16/20 count)
2 teaspoons	Bruno's Dry Adobo Seasoning
	(or Creole seasoning), or to taste
2 medium	fresh jalapeños, seeds removed, cut into ¼-inch thick strips
10 slices	thin-sliced smoked bacon (or turkey bacon), cut in half
	crosswise to make 20 short slices
	Sweet and Sour Dipping Sauce
	(see recipe on page 23), as an accompaniment

Special Equipment: 20 plain toothpicks

1. Peel, devein and butterfly the shrimp, leaving the tails intact. Sprinkle the shrimp with seasoning. Place one jalapeño strip down the center of each shrimp where they are butterflied. Starting at the head end, wrap the bacon evenly around the shrimp, being careful not to overlap the bacon. Secure the bacon with a toothpick, and then repeat with the remaining shrimp.

2. Preheat the grill to medium-high; clean and oil the grates to prevent sticking. Place the shrimp on the grill, and cook the first side until the bacon is crisp and brown, about 3 minutes. Flip the shrimp over and continue grilling until the shrimp are cooked through, about 3 minutes more. Remove the shrimp from the grill and serve hot or at room temperature with Sweet and Sour Dipping Sauce.

Vietnamese Summer Rolls with Fresh Crabmeat

Makes 12 summer rolls

2 ounces	bean thread vermicelli*
12 (12-inch)	dried rice paper rounds* (plus a few spares)
1 small bag	mixed baby greens
1 small	carrot, peeled and finely shredded
5 each	green onions, green tops only, very thinly sliced
1 pound	jumbo lump crabmeat
½ cup	whole fresh mint leaves
½ cup	whole fresh cilantro leaves
	Hoisin Peanut Sauce
	(recipe follows), as an accompaniment

1. Place the bean thread vermicelli in a medium bowl, and cover with lukewarm water for at least 2 hours and up to overnight. Drain thoroughly, and cut into 1-inch strands with kitchen scissors.

2. Dip each dried rice paper round into a shallow bowl of water, and spread them out among layers of damp, clean kitchen towels. Allow the wrappers to sit for 1 minute to soften.

3. Place one wrapper on a work surface; place a small amount of greens (about ¼ cup) on the lower half of the wrapper, leaving a ¾-inch border on the sides. Place a small amount of the rice vermicelli, carrots and green onions on top of the greens.

4. Fold the sides in, and begin to roll one turn from the bottom. Place several lumps of crabmeat and two or three mint and cilantro leaves on the roll, and continue to roll tightly. Press to seal.

5. Cut each roll in half diagonally, and serve with Hoisin Peanut Sauce.

Available at your local Asian market.

Louie's Note: These are fantastic for outdoor summer entertaining! If you would like to make vegetarian, just add asparagus, red bell peppers, yellow bell peppers and/or red onions. If you find that the rice paper is tearing, just use 2 sheets for each salad roll. And it you want to make it ahead of time, these rolls can be assembled up to 4 hours in advance. Just cover with wet paper towels and wrap tightly in plastic wrap.

Hoisin Peanut Sauce
Makes 1 cup

⅔ cup	hoisin sauce*
1 clove	garlic, minced
¼ cup	water
2 tablespoons	unseasoned rice vinegar*
¼ teaspoon	granulated sugar (or Splenda®)
1 tablespoon	finely chopped roasted peanuts, for garnish
1 tablespoon	very thinly sliced green onions, green tops only, for garnish

1. In a small saucepan, combine the hoisin sauce, garlic, water, vinegar and sugar. Bring to a boil, then reduce the heat and simmer until the mixture has thickened, about 8 to 10 minutes. Remove from the heat, and set aside to cool.

2. When the sauce has cooled, transfer into small sauce bowls and garnish with chopped peanuts and green onions.

Available at your local Asian market.

Crunchy Almonds
with Cayenne and Cumin
Serves 6

2 cups	whole blanched almonds
2 tablespoons	extra-virgin olive oil
½ teaspoon	cayenne pepper, or to taste
1 teaspoon	paprika
1 teaspoon	ground cumin
1 teaspoon	ground coriander
2 teaspoons	kosher salt, or to taste

1. Preheat the oven to 325 degrees F. In a medium bowl, toss the almonds with the olive oil, cayenne, paprika, cumin, coriander and salt.

2. Arrange the almonds on a baking sheet in a single even layer. Cook until golden brown, about 15 minutes. Remove from the oven, and set aside to cool completely.

3. Store in an airtight container or plastic zip-top bag for up to 2 weeks.

Curry Cashews
Serves 8

3 cups	cashews
2 tablespoons	extra-virgin olive oil
1½ teaspoons	ground cumin
1½ teaspoons	ground coriander
1½ teaspoons	ground turmeric
1½ teaspoons	kosher salt, or to taste
¼ teaspoon	cayenne pepper, or to taste
½ cup	raisins
½ cup	sweetened shredded coconut, toasted

1. Preheat the oven to 325 degrees F. In a medium bowl, toss the cashews with the olive oil, cumin, coriander, turmeric, salt and cayenne.

2. Arrange the cashews on a baking sheet in a single even layer. Cook until golden brown, about 20 minutes. Remove from the oven, and set aside to cool completely.

3. Add the raisins and coconut to the cashews, and toss to combine. Store in an airtight container or plastic zip-top bag for up to 2 weeks.

Vanilla Walnuts
Serves 8

1 large	vanilla bean
1 teaspoon	kosher salt, or to taste
¼ teaspoon	cayenne pepper, or to taste
½ teaspoon	ground cardamom
¼ teaspoon	ground cinnamon
¼ teaspoon	ground nutmeg
¼ teaspoon	ground allspice
1 pound	walnut halves (or pecan halves)
2½ tablespoons	canola oil
½ cup	granulated sugar (or Splenda®)

1. Slice the vanilla bean in half lengthwise, and scrape the seeds into a small bowl. Add the salt, cayenne, cardamom, cinnamon, nutmeg and allspice, stirring to combine. Set aside.

2. Preheat the oven to 325 degrees F. Boil the walnuts for 1 minute; drain, then place in a large bowl. While still warm, toss with the oil and sugar; set aside for 10 minutes.

3. Arrange the sugar-coated nuts on a rimmed baking sheet and cook until the nuts are very crisp and golden brown, about 30 minutes. Turn the nuts about every 10 minutes while cooking. Wipe the large bowl clean with paper towels.

4. Take the crispy brown nuts out of the oven, and pour into the large clean bowl; sprinkle the spice mixture over the nuts, and toss to coat well. Spread the nuts out in a single even layer on a clean baking sheet to cool completely before serving. Store in an airtight container at room temperature for up to 2 weeks.

Empanadas

Serves 6

Dough:

2¼ cups	all-purpose flour
½ teaspoon	kosher salt
½ cup	very cold lightly salted butter (or healthy butter alternative such as Smart Balance® Buttery Spread), cut into small chunks
⅓ cup	ice cold water, or more as needed
1 large	egg

Filling:

2 tablespoons	extra-virgin olive oil
½ cup	finely diced yellow onion
1 cup	finely diced red bell pepper
1 tablespoon	minced garlic
2 teaspoons	paprika
1 teaspoon	cayenne pepper, or to taste
1 teaspoon	dried oregano
1 tablespoon	Bruno's Dry Adobo Seasoning (or your favorite adobo), or to taste
1 pound	ground chuck (or ground turkey)
¼ cup	diced tomatoes (drained well if canned)
2 tablespoons	red wine vinegar
	salt and pepper, to taste
½ cup	finely diced queso blanco (or crumbled feta cheese)
1 cup	fresh cilantro leaves, chopped
1 tablespoon	capers, chopped
1	eggwash (1 large egg beaten with 1 tablespoon water)

For the Dough:

1. Preheat the oven to 350 degrees F. Combine the flour, salt and butter in a food processor; pulse until the dough is crumbly with pea-size pieces.

2. Add the cold water and egg, and pulse just until a ball of dough forms. Wrap in plastic wrap, and chill until needed.

For the Filling:

3. Place a medium sauté pan over medium heat; add the oil and heat through. Sauté the onions and peppers until soft, about 5 minutes. Add the garlic, paprika, cayenne, oregano and adobo and cook until fragrant, about 1 minute more.

4. Add the beef, tomatoes and vinegar and cook until all of the liquid is absorbed, about 5 minutes. Taste, and adjust the seasoning as needed with salt and pepper. Allow the mixture to cool completely, then stir in the cheese, cilantro and capers.

To Assemble the Empanadas:

5. Divide the dough into 6 equal balls. On a floured work surface, roll each ball into a ⅛- to ¼-inch thick disk that is about 6 inches in diameter. Put about ⅓ to ½ cup filling in the center of each disk, leaving a ½-inch border all the way around. Rub eggwash around the edges, and fold in half to enclose the filling. Use a fork to seal the edges. Prick the middle of each empanada once with a fork to release steam while baking.

6. Place the empanadas on a parchment paper-lined baking sheet, then brush the tops with egg wash. Bake until golden brown, about 30 to 35 minutes. Serve hot.

Whole-Wheat Baked Tortilla Chips

Serves 4

8 (8-inch)	whole-wheat tortillas
¼ cup	extra-virgin olive oil
1½ teaspoons	Bruno's Dry Adobo Seasoning
	(or Creole seasoning), or to taste
	vegetable oil cooking spray

1. Preheat the oven to 350 degrees F. Lightly brush the tortillas, front and back, with olive oil. Season generously with adobo.

2. Cut each tortilla round into 8 triangular wedges with kitchen scissors or a very sharp knife.

3. Spray 2 or 3 baking sheets lightly with vegetable oil cooking spray. Evenly spread the tortilla chips in a single layer. Bake, turning halfway through cooking time, until crisp and golden brown, about 15 minutes. Serve warm or at room temperature.

Sesame Pita Chips
Serves 6

6 rounds	whole-wheat pita bread
3 tablespoons	extra-virgin olive oil
	salt and pepper, to taste
2 tablespoons	white sesame seeds
2 tablespoons	black sesame seeds

1. Preheat the oven to 375 degrees F. Split the pita bread in half to make two, thin rounds; cut the rounds into triangles with a very sharp knife.

2. Place the triangles on a baking sheet, and brush both sides with olive oil; sprinkle the top side with salt, pepper and sesame seeds. Bake until very crisp, about 10 to 15 minutes; set aside to cool.

3. Serve the pita chips at room temperature with your favorite dip.

Crab Fritters
Serves 8

½ cup	coarsely chopped carrots
1 medium	red onion, coarsely chopped
½ cup	coarsely chopped celery
1 small	red bell pepper, stem, seeds and ribs removed, chopped
1 tablespoon	minced garlic
2 tablespoons	extra-virgin olive oil
2 tablespoons	Bruno's Dry Adobo Seasoning (or Creole seasoning), or to taste
1½ cups	all-purpose flour
1½ cups	whole-wheat flour
1 tablespoon	baking powder
1 cup	whole milk (or 2% milk)
2 large	eggs, beaten
1 pound	jumbo lump crabmeat
½ cup	shredded manchego cheese (or low-fat mozzarella)
	juice of 2 lemons
	hot sauce (such as Tabasco®), to taste
	salt and pepper, to taste
	canola oil, for frying
	Papaya Honey Mustard (see recipe on page 66), as an accompaniment

1. Combine the carrots, red onions, celery, bell pepper and garlic in a food processor; pulse until very finely chopped. (Do not over-process, or the vegetables will liquefy.)

2. Heat a medium sauté pan over medium-high heat; add the oil and heat through. Add the chopped vegetables and adobo, and sauté until tender, about 3 to 5 minutes. Strain off the excess liquid, and set aside to cool.

3. Whisk together the flours and baking powder in a medium mixing bowl. Stir in the milk, eggs and vegetable mixture; mix to thoroughly combine.

4. Gently fold in the crabmeat, cheese, lemon juice and hot sauce. Season to taste with salt and pepper.

5. In a deep fryer or large, deep sauté pan, heat the oil to 360 degrees F. Drop two tablespoons of batter into the oil to make a fritter, and fry until crispy and golden brown. (A one-ounce scoop works nicely.) Taste and adjust the seasoning as needed with salt and pepper. Continue making fritters until all of the fritter batter is gone. (Do not over-crowd the pan! Cook in batches.) Drain on paper towels.

6. If the fritters are not cooked all the way through when golden brown, place in a preheated 400 degree F oven and cook until done, about 3 minutes. Serve hot with Papaya Honey Mustard.

Louie's Note: I know when you hear "fritters" you think it's going to be fried and thighs are going to get WIDE. Well, these aren't really so bad – just control yourself and only have 3 or 4 fritters. It's a perfect cheat day recipe to share with a friend. Just remember to use healthy canola oil – and make sure the oil is hot enough so that the fritters do not soak up too much oil.

Mieng Kum

Serves 6 to 8

Sauce:

2 teaspoons	shrimp paste*
1 tablespoon	fish sauce* (preferably Squid brand)
1 (2-inch) piece	fresh ginger, peeled and crushed
1 cup	water
1½ cups	granulated sugar (or Splenda®)
1 whole	shallot, peeled and crushed

Mieng Kum:

1 medium	lime
6 cups	fresh spinach leaves, large stems removed
½ cup	unsweetened coconut, toasted
½ cup	roasted, salted peanuts
¼ cup	peeled fresh ginger, very finely diced
¼ cup	peeled fresh shallots, very finely diced
¼ cup	small dried shrimp*
5 to 6 whole	fresh Thai chiles,* very thinly sliced

For the Sauce:

1. Combine all of the sauce ingredients in a medium saucepan over medium-high heat. Bring to a boil, then reduce the heat and simmer until the sauce is thick and syrupy, about 15 to 20 minutes. Cool completely, then remove and discard the ginger and shallot; set aside.

For the Mieng Kum:

2. Slice the lime (do not peel) into ⅛-inch thick rounds. Slice the rounds into tiny wedges. Set aside.

3. To eat the mieng kum, make a tiny cup with a spinach leaf by folding the stem-end up about ¼ inch then pinching the sides of the leaf together.

4. Place equal amounts of coconut, peanuts, ginger, shallots, dried shrimp and lime wedges in the spinach cup; add 1 slice of chile, and top with a nice spoonful of sauce. Eat the whole parcel in one bite, and wait for the explosion of flavor. Wow! Continue making cups in this manner until all of the ingredients are gone.

Available at your local Asian market.

Thai Spring Rolls
with Sweet and Sour Dipping Sauce
Makes 25 spring rolls

4 ounces	bean thread vermicelli*
1 pound	ground pork (or ground turkey)
2 cloves	garlic, minced
2 teaspoons	granulated sugar (or Splenda®)
1 tablespoon	finely minced fresh ginger
3 tablespoons	fish sauce* (preferably Squid brand)
2 tablespoons	Maggi® Seasoning,* or to taste
1½ teaspoons	crushed red pepper flakes, or to taste
¼ cup	finely chopped fresh cilantro leaves
12 each	green onions, green tops only, very thinly sliced
1 small	carrot, peeled and finely grated
	salt and pepper, to taste
25 (6 x 6-inch)	frozen spring roll skins* (wrappers), thawed
1	egg wash (1 large egg beaten with 1 tablespoon water)
	canola oil, for frying
	Sweet and Sour Dipping Sauce
	(recipe follows), as an accompaniment

1. Place the bean thread vermicelli in a medium bowl, and cover with lukewarm water for at least 2 hours and up to overnight. Drain thoroughly, and cut into 1-inch strands with kitchen scissors.

2. Cook the ground pork in a medium sauté pan over medium-high heat until done. Drain, and return the meat back to the pan. Add the garlic, sugar, ginger, fish sauce, Maggi and crushed red pepper flakes, and cook for 1 to 2 minutes; set aside to cool completely.

3. Add the cilantro, green onions, carrots and chopped vermicelli to the cooled meat mixture, and stir to combine. Taste, and season as needed with salt and pepper.

4. Working with 1 wrapper at a time, place a portion of the filling in the bottom corner of the wrapper; fold over one end on the diagonal to form a triangle, then fold in the sides and roll up. Brush the edges with egg wash,

then gently squeeze the spring roll to seal the ends. Place the spring rolls on a parchment paper-lined baking sheet spaced 1-inch apart to prevent sticking together.

5. Heat the oil to 350 degrees F. Fry the spring rolls in a wok or large deep saucepan until crisp and golden brown, about 5 to 10 minutes. Drain on paper towels and serve hot with Sweet and Sour Dipping Sauce.

Sweet and Sour Dipping Sauce
Makes 1 cup

1 cup	distilled white vinegar
½ cup	granulated sugar (or Splenda®)
1 teaspoon	kosher salt
1 teaspoon	minced garlic
1 tablespoon	Sambal Oelek* (Asian chile sauce)

1. Simmer the vinegar and sugar in a small saucepan over medium-high heat until the sugar has completely dissolved and the mixture has reduced by one-third, about ten minutes.

2. Remove from the heat and stir in the salt, garlic and Asian chile sauce. Cool, and serve at room temperature. The sauce should be the consistency of light syrup.

*Available at your local Asian market

Thai Beef Lettuce Wraps with Thai Peanut Sauce

Serves 4

1 pound	lean ground beef (or ground bison or turkey)
3 tablespoons	fresh lime juice (about 2 limes)
1 tablespoon	fish sauce* (preferably Squid brand), or to taste
2 tablespoons	Maggi® Seasoning,* or to taste
¼ cup	whole mint leaves
¼ cup	whole cilantro leaves
4 each	green onions, green tops only, very thinly sliced
2 small	shallots, very thinly sliced
1 teaspoon	crushed red pepper flakes, or to taste
1 head	Bibb or green leaf lettuce, separated into individual leaves
	Thai Peanut Sauce
	(see recipe on page 3), as an accompaniment

1. Cook the beef over medium-high heat in a medium sauté pan until brown and cooked through; drain well, and place in a medium bowl.

2. Stir together the lime juice, fish sauce and Maggi; pour over the browned meat, and stir to combine.

3. Add the mint, cilantro, green onions, shallots and crushed red pepper flakes. Taste and adjust the seasoning as needed with fish sauce, Maggi and crushed red pepper flakes.

4. To serve, simply spoon about 2 ounces of the meat mixture into a chilled lettuce cup, and top with a small spoonful of Thai Peanut Sauce. Eat with your fingers as you would a taco.

Available at your local Asian market.

Piononos
(Stuffed Sweet Plantain Rolls)
Makes 6 piononos

Filling:

2 tablespoons	extra-virgin olive oil, divided
1 pound	ground chuck (or ground turkey)
1 teaspoon each	kosher salt and freshly ground black pepper, or to taste
½ medium	yellow onion, finely diced
½ medium	red bell pepper, stem, seeds and ribs removed, finely diced
2 teaspoons	minced garlic
1 each	bay leaf
1 tablespoon	chopped green olives
2 tablespoons	raisins

Plantains:

3 large	ripe plantains
	canola oil, for frying
3 large	eggs, beaten
½ cup	all-purpose flour
	salt and pepper, to taste

Special Equipment: toothpicks

For the Filling:

1. Place a large sauté pan over medium-high heat; add 1 tablespoon of the oil and heat through. Season the beef with the salt and pepper and cook until brown and cooked through, about 5 minutes; drain the beef in a colander, and set aside. Do not wipe out the pan.

2. Place the sauté pan back over medium heat; add the remaining oil and heat through. Cook the onions and bell peppers until tender, about 5 to 8 minutes; add the garlic, bay leaf, olives and raisins, and cook until the raisins are plumped, about 2 to 3 minutes more. Add the beef back to the pan, stirring to combine; set aside.

For the Plantains:

3. Peel and slice the plantains lengthwise into ¼-inch thick slices. (You should get four slices from an average plantain.) Fry the plantains a few at a time in 350 degree F oil until the plantains are very light golden brown. (Do not cook too long, or the plantains will become brittle.) Drain on paper towels until cool enough to handle.

26

4. For each pionono, take two fried plantain strips and shape into a circle, overlapping the strips on either side by about 1 inch. Secure with toothpicks. Fill each plantain ring with enough filling to completely fill the hole, and press together with your hands.

5. In a small bowl, combine the eggs, flour, salt and pepper. Dip the tops and bottoms (not the sides) of the piononos into the batter, then fry until golden brown, about 2 to 3 minutes per side. Drain on paper towels, then serve hot.

Louie's Note: My wife thought she had died and gone to heaven the first time my mother made these for her. She had never had anything like it. Piononos are a little bit time-consuming – but they are sure worth it!

Pear, Blue Cheese and Vanilla Walnut Canapés
Makes 22 canapés

1 (1-pound) loaf	thin pumpernickel bread*
3 to 4 tablespoons	extra-virgin olive oil
6 ounces	blue cheese, crumbled (about 1½ cups)
2 ounces	cream cheese (or reduced-fat cream cheese), brought to room temperature (¼ cup)
3 tablespoons	heavy cream (or 2% milk), or as needed
1 teaspoon	freshly ground black pepper
2 to 3 each	Cabernet-Poached Pears (see recipe on page 177)
1 recipe	Vanilla Walnuts (see recipe on page 13)

1. Preheat the oven to 350 degrees F. Cut the pumpernickel bread into bite-size rounds (1½ to 2-inch) with a canapé cutter. Brush both sides of each crouton liberally with olive oil, and place on a baking sheet. Cook until very crisp, about 25 to 35 minutes. Set aside to cool.

2. In an electric mixer with the paddle attachment, beat the blue cheese, cream cheese, cream and black pepper until the mixture is about the texture of peanut butter; if needed, add more cream to thin.

3. Cut the poached pears into ¼-inch thick slices; place on paper towels to drain briefly. If the pears are large, cut the slices in half to fit the canapés properly.

4. To assemble the canapés, spread a ¼-inch thick layer of blue cheese mixture on each crouton. Top each crouton with a slice of poached pear slightly off-center, then press one Vanilla Walnut into the cheese spread on the other side; serve immediately.

A 1-pound loaf of thin pumpernickel bread has 11 (4 x 4½-inch) slices. You can cut 2 (1½ or 2-inch) rounds out of each slice to make 22 canapés.

Louie's Note: The croutons may be made up to 3 days ahead of time; store at room temperature in an airtight container. The blue cheese spread may be made 3 days ahead of time; store, tightly covered, in the refrigerator. The pears may be made up to 5 days ahead of time; store refrigerated in their own poaching liquid.

Scallop Ceviche

Serves 8

2 pounds	large fresh sea scallops, quartered (or whole bay scallops)
½ cup	fresh lemon juice (about 3 lemons)
½ cup	fresh lime juice (about 6 limes)
½ cup	fresh orange juice (about 2 oranges)
¼ cup	finely diced red bell pepper
¼ cup	finely diced yellow bell pepper
¼ cup	finely diced red onion
½ cup	fresh cilantro leaves, coarsely chopped
3 each	green onions, green tops only, thinly sliced
	salt and pepper, to taste
	hot sauce (such as Tabasco®), to taste
	crackers, flatbread or lettuce cups, as an accompaniment

1. Bring a medium saucepan of salted water to a boil; add the scallops, and cook for one minute. Immediately plunge into a bowl of ice water; quickly drain the scallops, then pat dry with paper towel. (Do not over-cook, because the scallops will continue to "cook" in the citrus marinade. You don't want rubbery scallops!) Transfer the scallops to a large glass or stainless steel bowl to cool completely.

2. Pour the fresh citrus juices over the scallops; add the bell peppers, red onions, cilantro and green onions, and toss to coat. Season to taste with salt, pepper and hot sauce.

3. Place in the refrigerator and chill for at least 2 hours or up to overnight. Serve cold with crackers, flatbread or lettuce cups.

Black Bean Hummus with Tostones

Serves 6

3 tablespoons	extra-virgin olive oil
1 small	white or yellow onion, chopped
½ medium	red bell pepper, chopped
2 cloves	garlic, minced
1 teaspoon	dried oregano
1 teaspoon	ground cumin
2 (15-ounce) cans	black beans, drained and rinsed
3 tablespoons	tahini (ground sesame seed paste)
3 tablespoons	fresh lime juice (about 2 limes)
3 tablespoons	fresh cilantro leaves
2 teaspoons	hot sauce (such as Tabasco®), or to taste
1 tablespoon	Bruno's Dry Adobo Seasoning (or your favorite adobo), or to taste
	chicken broth or warm water, as needed to thin
	salt and pepper, to taste
4 each	green onions, green tops only, thinly sliced, for garnish
	Tostones (recipe follows), as an accompaniment

1. Place a medium sauté pan over medium-high heat; add the oil and heat through. Stir in the onions and bell peppers and cook until tender, about 10 minutes. Add the garlic, dried oregano and cumin, and cook two minutes more. Pour in the beans and cook until hot throughout, about 3 minutes.

2. Place the bean mixture and the tahini in a food processor, and pulse to combine. Add the lime juice, cilantro, hot sauce and adobo seasoning, and process until the dip is completely smooth. If the dip is too thick, add broth or water, one tablespoon at a time, until the desired consistency is achieved. Taste and adjust the seasoning as needed with salt, pepper and hot sauce.

3. Garnish with green onions, and serve at room temperature with Tostones. If not serving within an hour, store in an airtight container in the refrigerator for up to 3 days. Remove from the refrigerator 1 hour before serving.

Louie's Note: If you don't want to make Tostones, Whole-Wheat Baked Tortilla Chips (see recipe on page 16) will also be delicious with this dip.

Tostones
(Double Fried Plantains)
Serves 4

2 large	green plantains
2 cups	canola oil, or as needed
	salt and pepper, to taste

1. Peel the plantains,* then cut on the diagonal into ¾-inch thick slices.

2. Heat the oil to 375 degrees F in a large deep sauté pan; fry the plantain slices until tender but not crusty. Remove from the oil, and drain on paper towels.

3. Place the plantain slices on a clean work surface; cover with parchment paper, wax paper or a brown paper bag, and press down with the palms of your hands to flatten each fried plantain.

4. Fry the flattened plantains again until crusty and golden brown on both sides. Drain on paper towels, and season with salt and pepper. Serve hot.

To peel plantains, cut both ends off each plantain at an angle, then make one long shallow cut along the ridge of the plantain, being careful to not cut into the flesh. Run your fingers along the cut portion to slowly work off the peel. If you are really having trouble removing the peel, simmer the plantains for 3 to 5 minutes – the peels will slip right off!

Louie's Note: Tostones are one of my childhood favorites. They are terrific by themselves or with some Garlic and Cilantro Mojo (see recipe on page 35). Serve these with a Cuban Sandwich (see recipe on page 100) and a cup of Black Bean Soup (see recipe on page 43), and you'll feel like you're in Cuba.

Grilled Adobo-Rubbed Shrimp
with Garlic and Cilantro Mojo
Serves 6

2 pounds	jumbo shrimp (16/20 count), peeled and deveined, tails on
2 tablespoons	extra-virgin olive oil
3 tablespoons	Bruno's Dry Adobo Seasoning (or your favorite adobo), or to taste
1 medium	lemon, cut into wedges
	Garlic and Cilantro Mojo (recipe follows), as an accompaniment

Special Equipment: 6-inch bamboo skewers, soaked in water

1. Preheat the grill to medium-high; clean and oil the grates to prevent sticking.

2. In a large bowl, toss the shrimp with the oil and adobo to coat well. Arrange the shrimp on the soaked skewers, leaving a little bit of space between each shrimp.

3. Grill the skewers until the shrimp are pink, lightly charred and just cooked through, about 2 minutes per side.

4. To serve, slide the shrimp off the skewers (if desired) and arrange on a serving platter. Squeeze lemon juice over the shrimp, then drizzle with the Garlic and Cilantro Mojo. Serve warm or at room temperature with additional mojo and lemon wedges on the side.

Louie's Note: I love to use all-natural, sustainably-raised freshwater prawns from Lauren Farms in Leland, Mississippi. For more information about these sweet, succulent prawns, visit laurenfarms.com.

Garlic and Cilantro Mojo

½ cup	extra-virgin olive oil
8 cloves	garlic, minced
1 teaspoon	crushed red pepper flakes, or to taste
½ cup	fresh cilantro leaves, finely chopped
1 teaspoon	kosher salt, or to taste

1. Combine the olive oil, garlic and crushed red pepper flakes in a medium saucepan over medium-low heat; cook until the garlic is light golden brown, about 3 to 5 minutes. (Be careful not to burn the garlic!) Remove the pan from the heat, and set aside to cool.

2. Stir in the cilantro and salt; taste, and adjust the seasoning as needed with crushed red pepper flakes and salt. Serve hot or room temperature.

Bacalaitos
(Fried Salt Cod Fritters)
Serves 4

1 pound	dried salt cod (bacalao)*
2 cups	all-purpose flour
2 teaspoons	baking powder
1 tablespoon	Bruno's Dry Adobo Seasoning (or your favorite adobo)
1 tablespoon	Bruno's Citrus Herb Seasoning (or your favorite citrus seasoning)
1½ cups	water
1½ tablespoons	chopped fresh cilantro leaves
	canola oil, for frying

1. Soak the salt cod in cold water in the refrigerator overnight. Change the water several times to help remove the excess salt. Drain well, then rinse under cool running water.

2. Place the salt cod in a medium saucepan over medium-high heat; cover with water. Bring to a boil, then immediately reduce the heat and simmer for 10 to 12 minutes.

3. Remove the fish from the pan, and drain on paper towels. When cool enough to handle, remove the bones and skin, then shred the fish.

4. In a medium bowl, whisk together the flour, baking powder, adobo, citrus seasoning and water until smooth. Add the cilantro and shredded fish, and whisk to combine; set aside.

5. In a deep fryer or large, deep sauté pan, heat about 1 inch of oil to 360 degrees F. Drop 2 tablespoonfuls of batter into the hot oil to make a fritter, and fry until crispy and golden brown. (A one-ounce scoop works nicely.) Continue making fritters until all of the fritter batter is gone. (Do not over-crowd the pan! Cook in batches.) Drain on paper towels, and serve hot.

Available at your local Mediterranean market or online at tienda.com.

Soups & Salads

Chickpea and Chorizo Soup

Serves 8

1 tablespoon	extra-virgin olive oil
1 large	yellow onion, finely diced
1 large	red bell pepper, stem, seeds and ribs removed, finely diced
3 each	bay leaves
3 cloves	garlic, minced
8 ounces	fresh chorizo (see recipe on page 61 or purchase)
2 quarts	chicken broth (8 cups)
1 (14.5-ounce) can	petite diced tomatoes
2 (15-ounce) cans	chickpeas (garbanzo beans), drained and rinsed
	salt and pepper, to taste
	hot sauce (such as Tabasco®), to taste
2 tablespoons	fresh parsley leaves, chopped

1. Heat a medium saucepot over medium heat; add the oil and heat through. Stir in the onions, peppers and bay leaves, and cook until the onions are tender, about 5 minutes. Add the garlic and cook one minute more.

2. Add the chorizo and cook another 5 minutes. (Don't worry if it's not fully cooked, it will cook in the broth.)

3. Add the broth, tomatoes and chickpeas, and simmer until the soup has reduced and thickened, about 30 to 40 minutes. Season with salt, pepper and hot sauce; garnish with chopped parsley, and serve hot.

Louie's Note: I love this dish, because my mom adds something different just about every time. Sometimes she even adds pig feet! Yes, I love pig feet. But I have written the recipe to accommodate all of those non pig feet eaters. You really should try them though…you may like them!

Tom Yum Goong
(Shrimp and Lemongrass Soup)
Serves 4

3 stalks	lemongrass*
1 (4-inch) piece	fresh galangal*
8 each	kaffir lime leaves*
4 each	Thai fresh chiles,* or to taste
2 quarts	low-sodium chicken broth (8 cups)
1 pound	large shrimp (21/25 count), peeled and deveined, tails off
1 (8-ounce) can	straw mushrooms,* drained
½ cup	fish sauce* (preferably Squid brand), or to taste
½ cup	fresh lime juice (about 6 limes), or to taste
3 each	green onions, green tops only, thinly sliced
½ cup	whole fresh cilantro leaves
½ cup	whole fresh mint leaves
	Steamed Jasmine Rice (see recipe on page 144), as an accompaniment

1. Peel the tough outer layers off the lemongrass stalks. You're only going to use the white and pale green parts, so slice off the tough, woody tops and throw them away.

2. Slice the galangal on a sharp diagonal into 1-inch pieces.

3. Tear the kaffir lime leaves in half. Slice the chiles in half lengthwise, and remove the seeds if you prefer a milder broth.

4. Place the lemongrass, galangal, kaffir lime leaves and chiles on a square of cheesecloth that is big enough to hold it all. Form a pouch, and tie it with kitchen twine.

5. Put the pouch of aromatics in with the chicken broth in a medium saucepot; bring to a boil. Reduce the heat, and simmer until the aroma is absolutely heavenly, about 15 minutes.

6. Add the shrimp, and cook until just pink, about 1 minute; add the mushrooms, and cook 1 minute more.

7. Just before serving, stir in the fish sauce, lime juice, green onions, cilantro and mint. Remove the pot from the heat, and taste the broth. You should have an equal balance of spicy, salty and sour. Please don't stop now if the flavors are not balanced- add more lime juice, fish sauce and/or chiles to suit your personal taste!

8. Remove and discard the pouch, then ladle an equal amount of soup into 4 large bowls. Serve immediately with steamed jasmine rice.

Variation:

For Tom Kha Gai, substitute bite-size cubes of chicken for the shrimp, and replace 1 quart of the chicken broth with coconut milk (or light coconut milk).

Available at your local Asian market.

Louie's Note: For an explode-in-your-mouth, too good to be good-for-you broth, use fresh lemongrass, kaffir lime leaves and galangal. Now, if you don't know what any of this stuff is, don't worry about it. You're going to fall in love with these ingredients the same way that I did. You think I ate this stuff growing up in the Bronx? No way! And don't even tell me that you can't find fresh Thai produce. Just take a list of what you need to your local Asian market, and let them find it for you. They are happy to help. But if you do live in a really, really small town with no Asian market, you can always order online. My favorite online sources for Thai ingredients are listed at the back of this book.

Black Bean Soup

Makes about 3 quarts

1 pound	dried black beans*
2 quarts	beef broth (8 cups)
3 each	bay leaves
3 tablespoons	extra-virgin olive oil
½ cup	bacon (or turkey bacon), finely chopped
1 medium	yellow onion, finely diced
½ medium	red bell pepper, finely diced
3 cloves	garlic, minced
2 tablespoons	ground cumin
2 teaspoons	dried thyme
3 tablespoons	white vinegar
	hot sauce (such as Tabasco®), to taste
	salt and pepper, to taste
½ cup	fresh cilantro leaves, chopped

1. Pick through the beans for any stones or debris. Place in a colander, and rinse well under cool running water. Place the beans in a large stainless steel saucepot, and add the beef broth. Soak overnight.

2. Add the bay leaves to the saucepot, and place over medium-high heat; bring to a boil. Skim off any foam (scum) that forms at the top of the pot throughout the cooking process. Reduce the heat to a simmer, and cook until the beans are tender, about 2 to 3 hours. If necessary, add more broth to maintain the proper soup-like consistency.

3. Heat a sauté pan over medium heat; add the oil and heat through. Add the bacon and cook until crisp, about 5 minutes. Stir in the onions and peppers, and cook until soft, about 5 minutes; add the garlic, cumin and thyme, and cook until fragrant, about one minute more. Add the bacon-onion mixture to the beans.

4. Once the beans are tender add the vinegar, hot sauce, salt and pepper; simmer 30 minutes more. Just before serving, stir in the fresh cilantro. Taste, and adjust the seasoning as needed with hot sauce, salt and pepper. Serve hot.

* *The beans must be soaked in broth overnight.*

Louie's Note: Living in Florida for 3 years, I learned to put a little bit of chopped white onions on top of my beans. It's a nice touch. And don't worry about leftovers - you can make Black Bean Dip out of the soup!

Sopa de Mariscos

(Seafood Soup)

Serves 8

2 tablespoons	extra-virgin olive oil
1 large	yellow onion, diced
2 medium	red bell peppers, stems, seeds and ribs removed, diced
2 each	bay leaves
2 pinches	saffron
3 cloves	garlic, minced
1 teaspoon	chopped fresh thyme
1 cup	dry white wine
1 (14.5-ounce) can	diced tomatoes with juice
1 tablespoon	Bruno's Dry Adobo Seasoning (or your favorite adobo), or to taste
2 quarts	chicken broth (8 cups)
24 each	fresh littleneck clams, cleaned
24 each	fresh mussels, cleaned
1½ pounds	jumbo shrimp (16/20 count), peeled and deveined, tails off
½ pound	large sea scallops, quartered
	salt and pepper, to taste
2 tablespoons	chopped fresh cilantro leaves (optional)

1. Place a large saucepot over medium-high heat; add the olive oil and heat through. Stir in the onions, peppers, bay leaves, saffron, garlic and fresh thyme, and cook until the onions and peppers are tender, about 5 minutes.

2. Add the wine, stirring to get the brown bits off the bottom of the pan; cook until the wine has reduced by half. Add the tomatoes, adobo and broth; reduce the heat, and simmer for 30 minutes.

3. Add the clams and mussels, and simmer for 10 minutes. Add the shrimp and scallops and simmer until just cooked through, about 5 minutes more. Discard any clams or mussels that have not opened.

4. Taste, and adjust the seasoning as needed with salt and pepper. Stir in the cilantro, and serve immediately.

Sancocho

(Hangover Soup!)
Serves 8

3 tablespoons	extra-virgin olive oil, divided
1½ pounds	beef top round (or beef tenderloin), cut into ½-inch cubes
	salt and pepper, to taste
⅓ cup	diced yellow onions
⅓ cup	diced celery
⅓ cup	diced red bell peppers
3 each	bay leaves
1 tablespoon	minced garlic
4 medium	ripe red tomatoes, diced
3 quarts	beef broth (12 cups), divided
2 medium	green bananas, peeled and cut into 1-inch thick rounds
1 medium	yellow plantain, peeled and cut into 1-inch thick rounds
1 medium	sweet potato, peeled and cut into 1-inch cubes
½ pound	butternut squash, peeled and cut into 1-inch cubes
2 ears	fresh or frozen corn, cut into 1-inch thick rounds
¼ cup	fresh cilantro leaves, chopped

1. Place a large saucepot over medium heat; add 2 tablespoons of the oil and heat through. Add the beef and cook, stirring, until the beef is brown on all sides. Season with salt and pepper. Using a slotted spoon, put the browned beef in a bowl and set aside until needed.

2. Place the pot back over medium heat; add the remaining tablespoon of oil and heat through. Add the onions and cook until they begin to caramelize, about 10 minutes. Add the celery, bell peppers, bay leaves and garlic, and cook 3 minutes more. Season with salt and pepper.

3. Add the tomatoes and 1 quart of the beef broth, and simmer until the broth has reduced by half. Add the remaining beef broth, the beef, the green bananas, plantains, sweet potatoes, butternut squash and corn, and cook until the beef is tender and the vegetables are soft. Remove from the heat, and stir in the cilantro. Taste and season as needed with salt and pepper. Serve hot.

Louie's Note: I remember my mom making this every Christmas day. It was a special treat for the family members that didn't quite make it home after drinking a little too much the night before. But sometimes she just made it because it's so dadgum good!

Shrimp and Artichoke Salad

Serves 6

½ cup	white wine vinegar
2 tablespoons	Dijon mustard
¼ teaspoon each	kosher salt and freshly ground black pepper, or to taste
2 teaspoons	granulated sugar (or Splenda®), or to taste
¼ teaspoon	hot sauce (such as Tabasco®), or to taste
1 cup	extra-virgin olive oil
2 pounds large	peeled, deveined and cooked shrimp (21/25 count), tails off
2 (15-ounce) cans	artichoke hearts, drained and quartered
1 small bunch	green onions, green tops only, very thinly sliced
	your favorite lettuce, as an accompaniment (optional)

1. In a blender, combine the vinegar, mustard, salt, pepper, sugar and hot sauce; pulse to combine. With the motor running, add the oil in a slow, steady stream until the vinaigrette is creamy and emulsified. Taste and adjust the seasoning as needed with sugar, salt, pepper and hot sauce.

2. Combine the cooked shrimp, artichoke hearts and green onions in a large bowl; add the vinaigrette, and toss to combine. Serve over your favorite lettuce for a salad (or serve with toothpicks as a cocktail hors d'oeuvre).

Louie's Note: Great for a light lunch or for serving at a cocktail party.

Crispy Tomatoes
with Mozzarella and Fresh Thyme

Serves 4

2 cups	all-purpose flour (or whole-wheat flour)
	salt and pepper, to taste
2 large	eggs, beaten
¼ cup	heavy cream (or 2% milk)
1½ cups	Japanese breadcrumbs (panko)
	(or whole-wheat breadcrumbs)
3 medium	ripe but firm red tomatoes, sliced about ½-inch thick
	canola oil, for frying
8 ounces	fresh mozzarella, sliced ¼-inch thick
1 tablespoon	finely chopped fresh thyme

1. Place the flour on a plate, and season with salt and pepper. Set aside.

2. In a medium bowl, whisk together the eggs and cream; season with salt and pepper.

3. Place the breadcrumbs on a plate, and season with salt and pepper. One at a time, dredge each tomato slice in the seasoned flour, then dip in the egg mixture, then coat with the breadcrumbs.

4. Heat a large, non-stick sauté pan over medium to medium-high heat; add just enough oil to nicely coat the bottom of the pan, and heat through. Carefully add the breaded tomato slices to the oil, and cook until golden brown. Do not over-crowd the pan while frying – cook in batches.

5. When just about done, place the cheese slices on top of each fried tomato, and sprinkle with fresh thyme. Cover with a lid just until the cheese has melted; transfer to a paper towel-lined platter to drain briefly, then serve immediately.

Louie's Note: If you prefer to melt the cheese in the oven, just transfer the fried tomatoes to a baking sheet. Top with cheese and thyme and bake at 375 degrees F until the cheese has melted, about 3 to 5 minutes. This recipe will be great with Crabby Louie (recipe follows).

Crabby Louie

Serves 4

1 pound	jumbo lump crabmeat
¼ cup	mayonnaise (or light mayonnaise)
1 teaspoon	Sriracha Hot Chili Sauce* (a.k.a., Rooster Sauce)
	zest and juice of 2 lemons
	salt and pepper, to taste
¼ cup	finely diced red bell pepper
4 each	green onions, green tops only, thinly sliced at an angle
2 large	hard-boiled eggs, whites only, finely diced
1 medium	ripe red tomato, seeded and diced
1 medium	avocado, pitted, peeled and diced
	your favorite lettuce (Bibb, baby greens, etc.)

1. Carefully pick through the crabmeat for any shells or cartilage. Try to leave the lumps of crab as intact as possible. Set aside until needed.

2. In a small bowl, whisk together the mayonnaise, chili sauce, lemon zest and juice; season to taste with salt and pepper. Reserve half of the mayonnaise mixture, and leave the remainder in the bowl.

3. Add the red peppers, green onions, egg whites, tomatoes and avocados to the mayonnaise mixture in the bowl; toss to combine.

4. Gently fold in the crabmeat, being careful to distribute the ingredients evenly. Toss the lettuce with the reserved mayonnaise mixture, and divide among 4 chilled salad plates; top each with a spoonful of Crabby Louie, and serve immediately.

Sriracha may be found at your local Asian market or in the international section of larger supermarkets.

Louie's Note: Great served with some crunchy crostini.

Cuban Salad

Serves 4

½ head	iceberg lettuce, chopped into bite-size pieces
½ cup	small pimento-stuffed olives
3 medium	tomatoes, cut into wedges
½ cup	part-skim shredded mozzarella (2 ounces)
½ cup	grated manchego or Parmesan cheese (2 ounces)
1½ cups	croutons (or whole-wheat croutons)
1 tablespoon	Worcestershire sauce
¼ teaspoon	hot sauce (such as Tabasco®), or to taste
½ cup	Lemon Garlic Vinaigrette (recipe follows), or to taste
	salt and pepper, to taste

Combine all of the ingredients in a large salad bowl; toss to combine. Taste, and adjust the seasoning with hot sauce, salt and pepper. (The salad should be tangy and a little spicy!) Serve immediately.

Louie's Note: This salad recipe was given to me by a Cuban friend in Florida, and you will be surprised at how great it tastes. It's incredibly refreshing – addictive almost!

Lemon Garlic Vinaigrette
Makes about 3 cups

¾ cup	white vinegar
	zest of 6 lemons
½ cup	fresh lemon juice (about 6 lemons)
4 cloves	garlic, minced
¼ cup	granulated sugar (or Splenda®), or to taste
2 teaspoons	ground cumin
2 teaspoons	ground coriander
	salt and pepper, to taste
1½ cups	extra-virgin olive oil

1. Combine all of the ingredients except the olive oil in a blender. With the motor on low speed, slowly drizzle in the olive oil until creamy and emulsified.

2. Taste, and adjust the seasoning as needed with sugar, salt and pepper. If not using immediately store, tightly covered, in the refrigerator for up to 3 days.

Fresh Spinach Salad with Salsa and Shredded Manchego
Serves 4

6 cups	fresh spinach leaves
½ cup	cooked and crumbled turkey bacon
1 cup	Roasted Corn Salsa (see recipe on page 55)
¼ cup	shredded manchego cheese (or shredded Parmesan or crumbled goat cheese) (1 ounce)
20 to 24	baked pita chips, as an accompaniment

1. In a medium bowl, toss together the spinach, bacon, salsa and cheese.

2. Divide the salad evenly between 4 chilled salad plates, then arrange 5 or 6 pita chips on each salad; serve immediately.

Louie's Note: You can purchase salsa or you can enjoy homemade. This salad was a real life-saver when I was losing my weight. I would have a big bowl of spinach and have no worries - and I would be full until my next meal.

Asparagus Salad
with Roasted Peppers and Capers
Serves 4

2 tablespoons	red wine vinegar
½ teaspoon	creole mustard
⅛ teaspoon each	kosher salt and freshly ground pepper, or to taste
1 tablespoon	extra-virgin olive oil
1 tablespoon	chopped fresh parsley, divided
2 tablespoons	chopped shallots, divided
1 teaspoon	minced garlic
¼ cup	finely chopped roasted red peppers
¼ cup	finely chopped tomatoes
1 tablespoon	small capers
1 pound	asparagus spears, steamed until tender but crisp

1. In a medium bowl, whisk together the red wine vinegar, mustard, salt and pepper. Slowly whisk in the oil until creamy and emulsified.

2. Add ½ tablespoon parsley, ½ tablespoon shallots, the garlic, roasted red peppers, tomatoes and capers, and toss to combine. Taste, and adjust the seasoning as needed with salt and pepper.

3. Place the steamed asparagus in a shallow serving dish, and toss with the roasted red pepper mixture. Garnish with the remaining parsley and shallots, and serve at room temperature.

Louie's Note: Great for a ladies' luncheon!

Thai Grilled Eggplant Salad

Serves 6

2 medium	globe eggplants, peeled and cut into ½-inch thick rounds
4 tablespoons	canola oil, divided
2 small	poblano peppers, stems, seeds and ribs removed, finely diced
2 small	jalapeño peppers, stems, seeds and ribs removed, finely diced
1 large	yellow onion, finely diced
2 teaspoons	minced fresh garlic
4 medium	shallots, minced
½ cup	whole fresh cilantro leaves
½ cup	whole fresh mint leaves
2 tablespoons	dried shrimp* (optional)
	juice of 2 limes, or to taste, plus lime wedges for garnish
	fish sauce* (preferably Squid brand), to taste (optional)
	Bibb or green leaf lettuce, as an accompaniment

1. Preheat the grill to medium-high; clean and oil the grates to prevent sticking. Brush the eggplant slices on both sides with about 2 tablespoonfuls of the oil. Grill the eggplant until slightly charred on the outside and completely cooked through but not mushy, about 2 to 3 minutes per side. If necessary, turn down the grill heat to prevent burning.

2. Set the grilled eggplant on a paper towel-lined platter. When cool enough to handle, finely dice the eggplant and place in a medium bowl.

3. Heat a medium sauté pan over medium-high heat; add the remaining 2 tablespoons of oil and heat through. Sauté the poblano peppers, jalapeños and onions until tender, about 5 minutes. Add the garlic, and cook 1 minute more. Add the sautéed vegetables to the bowl with the diced eggplant, and stir to mix well.

4. Add the shallots, cilantro, mint, dried shrimp (if using), lime juice and fish sauce to the eggplant mixture, and mix well. Taste, and adjust the seasoning as needed with lime juice and fish sauce.

5. Serve with lettuce cups along with lime wedges and extra fish sauce on the side. To eat, spoon some eggplant salad into a lettuce cup; season as desired, and eat like a taco.

Available at your local Asian market.

Roasted Corn Salsa
Makes 1 quart

5 ears	fresh corn, unhusked
2 cups	cherry tomatoes, cut in half
1 small	red onion, cut into thin strips (or finely diced)
2 tablespoons	extra-virgin olive oil
2 tablespoons	Bruno's Citrus Herb Seasoning (or lemon pepper seasoning), or to taste
½ cup	crumbled feta cheese (2 ounces)
½ cup	whole fresh cilantro leaves
1 small bunch	green onions, green tops only, very thinly sliced
	juice of 3 limes
	salt and pepper, to taste
	hot sauce (such as Tabasco®), to taste

1. Preheat the grill to medium-high. Clean and oil the grates to prevent sticking. Grill the corn with the husk on until tender, about 15 to 20 minutes; turn every 3 minutes to make sure it is evenly cooked. (Note: The cornhusks will get charred, but don't worry – the corn will not be burnt.) Remove the corn from the grill; when cool enough to handle, remove the husks and silk.

2. Cut the corn kernels off the cobs into a medium bowl. Add the tomatoes, onions, oil, citrus seasoning, feta, cilantro, green onions, lime juice, salt, pepper and hot sauce; toss to mix gently. Taste, and adjust the seasoning as needed with salt, pepper and hot sauce. Serve at room temperature.

3. If not serving immediately, store tightly covered in the refrigerator for up to 3 days.

Louie's Note: This recipe is my brother Bob's favorite – he loves to serve it with grilled ribeyes that have been seasoned with Bruno's Dry Adobo Seasoning.

Honey Lemongrass Vinaigrette

Makes 3 cups

½ cup	honey
3 stalks	lemongrass,* chopped
½ medium	yellow bell pepper, stem, seeds and ribs removed
1 small	jalapeño, stem, seeds and ribs removed
1 (2-inch) piece	ginger, peeled and chopped
¼ cup	Spanish sherry vinegar
1 small	shallot, peeled
1 cup	canola oil
	salt and pepper, to taste

1. Combine all of the ingredients in a blender; mix on high speed until completely pulverized, smooth and creamy, about 3 minutes. Taste and adjust the seasoning with salt and pepper.

2. Strain the dressing through a coarse sieve into a medium bowl; press the pulp with a rubber spatula or a spoon to release as much liquid from the pulp as possible.

3. Discard the pulp, and store the dressing in the refrigerator in an airtight container for up to 3 days.

Use only the tender pale green tips of the lemongrass stalk. Remove and discard the tough outer leaves.

Louie's Note: What I love about this dressing is that it is one of those recipes where you can put everything in the blender and let it rip. You can refrigerate the dressing for up to 3 days, but after that you will start losing the fresh, citrusy lemongrass flavor.

Roasted Garlic Vinaigrette

Makes 1 cup

3 large heads	fresh garlic
½ cup	extra-virgin olive oil, divided
¼ cup	red wine vinegar
2 tablespoons	honey (or Splenda®)
	juice of 1 lime
	salt and pepper, to taste

1. Preheat the oven to 350 degrees F. Cut off the top ⅓ of the garlic heads without peeling. Drizzle 2 teaspoons of olive oil over the garlic bulbs, and wrap in aluminum foil. Place on a baking sheet and cook until soft throughout, about 45 minutes to an hour. If the garlic has not browned slightly, remove the foil and allow to cook, uncovered, for another 5 minutes or so.

2. Remove the roasted garlic from the oven and allow to cool; when cool enough to handle, squeeze the roasted garlic pulp out of the garlic heads. Set aside.

3. Combine the roasted garlic, vinegar, honey and lime juice in a blender. With the motor running, slowly drizzle in the remaining oil until creamy and emulsified.

4. Taste, and adjust the seasoning with salt and pepper as needed.

5. If not using immediately store, tightly covered, in the refrigerator for up to 3 days.

Louie's Note: If you add about 3 anchovies, ¼ cup of Parmesan cheese and 1 cup of fat-free mayo, you have a Roasted Garlic Caesar Dressing. Delicious!

Roasted Tomatillo and Garlic Soup with Whole-Wheat Baked Tortilla Chips and Avocado-Lime Crema

Serves 8

2 pounds	fresh tomatillos, husks removed
1 large	yellow onion, peeled and quartered
3 medium	yellow bell peppers
6 large cloves	garlic
¼ cup	extra-virgin olive oil
	salt and pepper, to taste
1 quart	chicken broth (4 cups)
	juice of 2 limes
1 tablespoon	ground cumin
1 tablespoon	white vinegar
1 teaspoon	granulated sugar (or Splenda®)
	hot sauce (such as Tabasco®), to taste
	Avocado-Lime Crema (see recipe on page 102)
	Whole-Wheat Baked Tortilla Chips (see recipe on page 16)

1. Preheat the oven to 400 degrees F. Combine the tomatillos, onions, bell peppers and garlic in a large mixing bowl; add the oil, and toss to coat. Season to taste with salt and pepper, then place in a roasting pan and cook until tender and golden brown, about 20 minutes.

2. Remove the roasted vegetables from the oven, and place in a large, heavy-duty plastic zip-top bag to further steam and soften them. When cool, remove the stems, skins and seeds from the bell peppers.

3. Meanwhile, simmer the chicken broth over medium heat in a medium saucepot. Add the roasted vegetables to the simmering broth, and simmer for 30 minutes.

4. Using a regular or hand-held blender, puree the soup until smooth. Add the lime juice, cumin, vinegar, sugar, salt, pepper and hot sauce, and puree to combine. Let simmer for another 10 to 15 minutes, then taste, and adjust the seasoning as needed with salt, pepper and hot sauce. Garnish with Avocado-Lime Crema, and serve with Whole-Wheat Baked Tortilla Chips.

Poultry

Bruno's Arroz con Pollo

Serves 8

Chicken:

1 whole	chicken, cut into 10 pieces (cut breasts in half)
3 tablespoons	extra-virgin olive oil, divided
¼ cup	Bruno's Dry Adobo Seasoning (or Creole seasoning), or to taste
½ cup	fresh cilantro leaves, chopped

Rice:

1 medium	yellow onion, diced
1 tablespoon	minced garlic
½ cup	pimento-stuffed green olives
1 tablespoon	small capers
4 ounces	fresh chorizo (recipe follows or purchase)
2 cups	long-grain white rice (or Uncle Ben's® Natural Whole-Grain Brown Rice)
2 teaspoons	saffron, chopped
4 cups	chicken broth
	hot sauce (such as Tabasco®), to taste
	salt and pepper, to taste
½ cup	thawed frozen green peas
1 (6-ounce) jar	roasted red peppers, sliced into thin strips, for garnish
¼ cup	fresh cilantro leaves, chopped, for garnish

For the Chicken:

1. Rub the chicken with one tablespoon of the olive oil, the adobo and the cilantro; place in the refrigerator, covered, and marinate for at least 3 hours or up to overnight.

2. Place a medium paella pan (or a deep wide saucepot) over medium-high heat; add the remaining oil and heat through. Add the chicken and sear on all sides until dark golden brown, about 5 minutes. Transfer the chicken to a plate, and tent with foil. Do not wipe out the pan

For the Rice:

3. Place the same pan back over medium heat. Add the onions, garlic, olives and capers, and cook for about 3 minutes; add the chorizo and cook 3 minutes more. Stir in the rice and saffron, mixing well to combine.

4. Add the chicken broth and hot sauce, stirring to combine. Taste, and adjust the seasoning as needed with salt and pepper. (Remember, capers and olives will contribute saltiness to the dish.) Arrange the seared chicken pieces on top of the rice; do not stir.

5. Cook, uncovered, over medium heat until the broth has evaporated, about 25 to 30 minutes; do not stir while cooking. Once the broth has evaporated, turn off the heat, add the peas, and cover the pan with a lid. Let sit, covered, for about 15 minutes.

6. When the rice is done, garnish with roasted red peppers and cilantro; serve hot.

Chorizo

Makes 2 pounds chorizo or 8 (4-ounce) patties

2 pounds	ground pork (or ground turkey)
¼ cup	Bruno's Dry Adobo Seasoning (or your favorite adobo)
2 tablespoons	water
¼ cup	red wine vinegar
	salt and pepper, to taste

1. In medium mixing bowl, combine all ingredients and mix very well.

2. Refrigerate or freeze until needed. (If desired, make eight 4-ounce patties and freeze separately; use when needed.)

Louie's Note: To test the seasoning in your chorizo, make a bite-size patty and cook in a small pan or in the microwave until just cooked through. Taste, and adjust the seasoning in the chorizo as needed. Continue making test patties until the seasoning is just right. By the way, chorizo is great for breakfast with some scrambled eggs or in an omelet with a little salsa on top!

Asian Sesame Noodles
with Chicken and Broccoli

Serves 4

Noodles:

½ pound	Chinese egg noodles* (or whole-wheat spaghetti)
2 teaspoons	kosher salt
4 quarts	cool water (16 cups)

Sauce:

3 tablespoons	toasted sesame oil*
1 (2½-inch) piece	fresh ginger, peeled and finely minced
2 cloves	garlic, minced
1 teaspoon	crushed red pepper flakes, or to taste
¼ cup	unsweetened rice vinegar*
½ cup	soy sauce (or low-sodium soy sauce)
2 teaspoons	granulated sugar (or Splenda®)
3 tablespoons	white sesame seeds
2 tablespoons	cornstarch

To Serve:

1 pound	fresh broccoli florets (about 2 cups)
¼ cup	fresh lime juice (about 3 limes)
1 pound	shredded cooked rotisserie chicken (see Louie's Note)
3 each	green onions, green tops only, thinly sliced, for garnish
2 tablespoons	black sesame seeds, for garnish
¼ cup	fresh cilantro leaves, for garnish

For the Noodles:

1. Boil the noodles in salted water until al dente (tender but firm to the bite). Drain, then rinse under cold running water; set aside.

For the Sauce:

2. Whisk together the sesame oil, ginger, garlic, crushed red pepper flakes, rice vinegar, soy sauce, sugar, sesame seeds and cornstarch. Set aside.

To Serve:

3. Place a wok over high heat, and add about ½ cup of water. Place the broccoli in the wok, stems down, and cook just until the water evaporates and the stems are almost tender, about 2 to 3 minutes.

4. Whisk the sauce again, then pour into the wok; cook, tossing and stirring constantly (stir-frying), until the sauce is thick and glossy, about 3 minutes. Add the noodles and lime juice, and toss to coat.

5. Mound the noodles in four individual pasta bowls; top each with an equal portion of chicken. Garnish with green onions, black sesame seeds and cilantro, and serve hot, warm or at room temperature.

Available at your local Asian market.

Louie's Note: Purchase a fully cooked rotisserie chicken; remove and discard the skin, then pull the meat from the bones and shred. Reserve the remaining chicken for another use - like chicken salad or soup.

Grilled Adobo Chicken with Chimichurri

Serves 6

6 (8-ounce)	boneless, skinless chicken breasts
2 tablespoons	extra-virgin olive oil
¼ cup	Bruno's Dry Adobo Seasoning (or your favorite adobo)
2 cups	Chimichurri Sauce (recipe follows), as an accompaniment

1. Preheat the grill to medium-high; clean and oil the grates to prevent sticking. Toss the chicken in the olive oil, then season generously on both sides with adobo.

2. Grill until nicely charred and cooked through, about 4 minutes per side or until an instant-read thermometer registers 165 degrees F in the thickest part of the breast.

3. Remove the breasts from the grill, and allow to rest for a couple of minutes. Slice each breast at an angle into ¼-inch thick slices; arrange on a platter, and serve with Chimichurri Sauce.

Chimichurri

Makes 1½ cups

1 (packed) cup	fresh cilantro leaves
¼ (packed) cup	fresh oregano leaves
1 (packed) cup	fresh parsley leaves
2 medium	jalapeño peppers, stems and seeds removed
4 cloves	garlic, peeled
¼ cup	white vinegar
	juice of 3 lemons
½ cup	extra-virgin olive oil
	salt and pepper, to taste

1. Combine all of the ingredients in a food processor; mix until smooth, about 3 minutes. Taste, and adjust the seasoning as needed with salt and pepper.

2. If not using immediately, store tightly covered in the refrigerator for up to 8 hours.

Louie's Note: Try this with grilled beef or pork tenderloin.

Sambal Chicken
Serves 4

4 (8-ounce)	boneless, skinless chicken breasts, cut into bite-size chunks
1 teaspoon	ground turmeric
	salt and pepper, to taste
¼ cup	canola oil
3 tablespoons	Sambal (see recipe on page 111)
1 medium	yellow onion, finely diced
1 (14.5-ounce) can	petite diced tomatoes
2 tablespoons	ketchup (or reduced-sugar ketchup)
1½ teaspoons	Knorr® Tamarind Soup Base*
1 tablespoon	granulated sugar (or Splenda®)
	Steamed Jasmine Rice (see recipe on page 144), as an accompaniment
	sliced fresh cucumbers, as an accompaniment (optional)

1. Season the chicken with turmeric, salt and pepper; set aside.

2. Heat a medium wok or sauté pan over medium-high heat; add the oil and heat through. Cook the chicken, stirring and tossing constantly (stir-frying), until golden brown, about 3 minutes. Transfer the chicken to a plate, and set aside until needed.

3. Add the Sambal and onions, and stir-fry until the onions are almost tender, about 3 minutes. Add the browned chicken, tomatoes, ketchup, tamarind and sugar, and simmer until the chicken is just cooked through.

4. Taste, and season as needed with salt and pepper. Serve with steamed jasmine rice and fresh sliced cucumbers, if desired.

Available at your local Asian market.

Papaya Honey Mustard Baked Chicken
Serves 6

	vegetable oil cooking spray, as needed
1 cup	Papaya Honey Mustard (recipe follows)
6 (6-ounce)	boneless, skinless chicken breasts
	salt and pepper, to taste
2 cups	corn flakes, crushed

1. Preheat the oven to 400 degrees F. Spray a baking sheet with vegetable oil cooking spray, and set aside.

2. In a large bowl, combine the Papaya Honey Mustard and chicken breasts; toss to coat, then season with salt and pepper.

3. Place the corn flakes in a separate bowl; press the chicken into the corn flakes, making sure to completely coat each breast.

4. Bake the chicken until just cooked through or until an instant-read thermometer registers 165 degrees F when inserted into the thickest part of the breast, about 15 to 20 minutes. Serve hot!

Papaya Honey Mustard
Makes 2 cups

2 medium	fresh ripe papayas, peeled, seeded and diced
½ cup	honey
	juice of 2 limes
½ cup	Creole mustard
½ cup	yellow mustard
	salt and pepper, to taste

Combine all of the ingredients in a blender; mix until smooth. If not using immediately, store, tightly covered, in the refrigerator for up to 5 days.

Louie's Note: I love to eat this chicken dish at home with some Roasted Sweet Potato Fries (see recipe on page 140). And the Papaya Honey Mustard is also delicious with grilled chicken or pork.

Chiles Rellenos
(Stuffed Chiles)
Serves 8

8 medium	poblano peppers
2 tablespoons	extra-virgin olive oil
½ small	red onion, finely diced
2 medium	zucchini (unpeeled), finely diced
½ teaspoon	ground cumin
½ teaspoon	ground oregano
1 teaspoon	minced garlic
1 (15-ounce) can	diced tomatoes, drained
1 (4-ounce) can	diced green chilies, drained
1 cup	corn kernels, fresh or thawed frozen
2 cups	diced cooked chicken
2 cups	cooked brown rice
1 cup	queso fresco (or low-fat Cheddar cheese)
	salt and pepper, to taste
	Mole Negro* (see recipe on page 70), as an accompaniment

1. Place a wire rack over a low-lit stovetop gas burner (or use your outdoor grill). Roast the poblano peppers on the rack, turning with tongs until blackened evenly. Place in a small bowl, and cover with plastic wrap; allow to steam in its own heat. Set aside until needed.

2. Heat a medium sauté pan over medium heat; add the oil and heat through. Add the onion and zucchini and sauté until tender, about 5 minutes. Add the cumin, oregano, garlic, tomatoes, green chiles and corn. Continue to cook, stirring occasionally, until the mixture is almost dry. Remove the pan from the heat. Place the mixture in a bowl to cool.

3. Add the chicken, rice and cheese, stirring to combine. Season to taste with salt and pepper, then set aside until needed.

4. Meanwhile, use a paper towel to rub the blistered skins off the roasted poblano peppers. Make an incision on one side of each poblano, then remove the seeds and membranes from inside, making sure to keep the peppers intact.

5. Heat the oven to 350 degrees F; while the oven is heating, stuff your peppers with the rice mixture. Bake until warmed through, about 15 to 20 minutes. Serve hot with the mole sauce.

Louie's Note: I love this recipe, because it has a little bit of everything - vegetables, rice and cheese. You can't ask for anything better. And I love the Mexican flair! The mole really gives a kick, but if you prefer, you may substitute your favorite salsa.

You can purchase prepared Mole Sauce in the international section of most grocery stores or at your local Spanish market.

Mole Negro
Makes about 6 cups

¼ pound	guajillo chiles, stemmed and seeded
¼ pound	pasilla chiles, stemmed and seeded
¼ pound	ancho chiles, stemmed and seeded
1 small	yellow onion, peeled and quartered
1 medium	tomato, quartered
4 medium	tomatillos, husked
5 large cloves	garlic, peeled
2 tablespoons	raisins
¼ cup	dried apricots
¼ cup	prunes (dried plums)
½ cup	dry red wine
1 tablespoon	dried oregano
2 teaspoons	cumin seeds
2 teaspoons	fennel seeds
2 teaspoons	whole black peppercorns
2 medium	cinnamon sticks
1½ teaspoons	kosher salt, or to taste
3 cups	chicken broth
2 tablespoons	dark brown sugar (or Splenda® brown sugar), or to taste
1 ounce	Mexican chocolate (or dark chocolate)
3 each	corn tortillas

1. Preheat the oven to 500 degrees F. Place all of the dried chilies on a baking sheet, and cook until fragrant, about 2 minutes. Immediately remove the toasted chiles from the oven, and submerge in a bowl of simmering water; set aside.

2. Preheat the broiler to high; place the onions, tomatoes, tomatillos and garlic on the baking sheet, and place in the oven. Cook until the vegetables are nicely charred but not burnt, about 5 minutes. Remove from the oven, and set aside. (Watch the garlic closely - you may need to remove it sooner.)

3. Combine the raisins, apricots, prunes and red wine in a small saucepan over medium heat; cook until the fruit has plumped, about 10 minutes; set aside.

4. Combine the oregano, cumin seeds, fennel seeds, black peppercorns and cinnamon sticks in a small sauté pan over medium-high heat; cook, stirring, until fragrant, about 1 minute. Cool slightly, then grind in a spice grinder; set aside.

5. To Assemble the Mole: Remove the toasted chiles from the water, and place in a medium saucepan; discard the soaking liquid. Add the charred vegetables, dried fruit and red wine mixture, toasted spices, salt and chicken broth to the pan; simmer over medium-low heat for 30 minutes.

6. Add the brown sugar, chocolate and tortillas, and simmer 15 minutes more. Remove the sauce from the heat, and puree in a blender until completely smooth* (you may need to do this in batches). Taste, and adjust the seasoning as needed with sugar and salt – you may need more of both.

7. If not serving the mole immediately, cool completely then store in an airtight container, refrigerated, for up to 1 week or in the freezer for up to 3 months.

Use caution when pureeing hot liquids. Fill the blender no more than halfway full, and cover the lid with a kitchen towel.

Louie's Note: Serve this very complex sauce with simply prepared chicken, beef or lamb. It's even delicious on grilled vegetables!

Grilled Jerk Chicken
with Mango Chutney

Serves 6

½ cup	Bruno's Caribbean Jerk Seasoning (or your favorite jerk seasoning)
1 medium	yellow onion, chopped
1 small bunch	green onions
1 teaspoon	crushed red pepper flakes, or to taste
1 tablespoon	minced garlic
1 (1-inch) piece	fresh ginger, peeled and coarsely chopped
1 tablespoon	fresh thyme leaves
1 small bunch	fresh cilantro, leaves and stems
½ cup	molasses
¼ cup	granulated sugar (or Splenda®)
	juice of 2 limes
¼ cup	malt vinegar (or red wine vinegar)
	salt and pepper, to taste
6 (8-ounce)	boneless, skinless chicken breasts
	Mango Chutney (recipe follows), as an accompaniment

1. Combine all of the ingredients except the chicken and chutney in a blender; mix until smooth. Place the chicken breasts in a large zip-top bag; add the jerk marinade and squeeze the bag to coat the chicken evenly. Seal the bag, place in the refrigerator, and marinate for at least 2 hours and up to overnight.

2. Preheat the grill to medium-high; clean and oil the grates to prevent sticking. Shake off the excess marinade, then grill until the internal temperature registers 165 degrees F in the thickest part of the breast, about 4 to 6 minutes on each side.

3. Remove the breasts from the grill, and allow to rest for a couple of minutes. Slice each breast at an angle into ¼-inch thick slices, and serve hot or at room temperature with Mango Chutney.

Louie's Note: This recipe may appear hard to make, but it's really quick and easy. If you prefer to purchase your chutney, you can find great ones at gourmet shops, Indian markets – or even supermarkets.

Mango Chutney

Makes 3 cups

4 medium	ripe fresh mangos, peeled and diced (or the equivalent thawed frozen mangos)
½ cup	apple cider vinegar
½ cup	fresh orange juice
1 cup	light brown sugar (or Splenda® brown sugar)
	zest and juice of 2 limes
2 teaspoons	finely minced fresh ginger
1 teaspoon	minced fresh garlic
1 small	yellow onion, finely diced
¼ teaspoon	cayenne pepper, or to taste
1 teaspoon	ground allspice
1 teaspoon	Worcestershire sauce
	salt and pepper, to taste

Combine all of the ingredients in a medium saucepan over medium-low heat. Simmer, stirring occasionally, until the mixture has reduced by half. Taste and adjust the seasoning as needed with salt and pepper. Serve hot or at room temperature.

Big Louie Sandwich with Spicy Basil Guacamole

Serves 4

¼ cup	dried Italian herbs
1 tablespoon	kosher salt, or to taste
1 teaspoon	freshly ground black pepper, or to taste
1 cup	water
¼ cup	extra-virgin olive oil
4 large	portobello mushrooms, gills removed (see Louie's Note)
1 medium	red onion, sliced into rings
2 medium	red bell peppers, stems, seeds and ribs removed, quartered
4 (6-ounce)	boneless, skinless chicken breasts
4 (6-inch)	hoagie rolls (or whole-wheat rolls), toasted or grilled
1 cup	Spicy Basil Guacamole (recipe follows)
1 cup	crumbled blue cheese (or your favorite cheese)(4 ounces)
2 cups	mixed baby greens (or your favorite lettuce)

1. In a large bowl, whisk together the herbs, salt, pepper, water and oil. Add the mushrooms, red onions and bell peppers, and toss to coat. Set aside until needed.

2. Preheat the grill to high. Clean and oil the grates to prevent sticking. Season the chicken with salt and pepper on both sides; grill until nicely charred and cooked through, about 4 minutes per side or until an instant-read thermometer registers 165 degrees F in the thickest part of the breast.

3. Remove the chicken from the grill. Cool completely, then cut each breast in half lengthwise to make two, thin even slices. (Note: Each sandwich will have 2 three-ounce slices of chicken.)

4. Clean and oil the grill again, then grill the vegetables until nicely charred and cooked through, about 3 to 5 minutes per side. Place the grilled vegetables in a clean bowl, and cover tightly with plastic wrap; they will continue to steam and soften as they cool.

5. Grill the rolls quickly - just enough to give them grill marks. To assemble a sandwich, spread 2 tablespoons of Spicy Basil Guacamole on the bottom and top roll. Place a grilled Portobello on the bottom roll, then add one-fourth of the grilled peppers and onions. Top with two grilled chicken slices and one-fourth of the blue cheese and lettuce. Cover with the top roll, then repeat with the remaining ingredients to make 4 BIG sandwiches. Serve immediately.

Spicy Basil Guacamole

Makes about 2½ cups

3 medium	ripe avocados (preferably Hass), pitted, peeled and chopped
1 clove	garlic, minced
1 medium	ripe red tomato, seeded and coarsely chopped
	juice of 1 lime
	juice of 1 lemon
2 each	green onions, thinly sliced
3 tablespoons	finely chopped fresh basil leaves
1 teaspoon	crushed red pepper flakes, or to taste
1 teaspoon	kosher salt, or to taste
¼ teaspoon	freshly ground black pepper, or to taste

1. In a large mixing bowl, mash 1 of the chopped avocados with a fork. Add the remaining chopped avocados, garlic, tomatoes, lime juice, lemon juice, green onions, basil, crushed red pepper flakes, salt and pepper; stir to combine.

2. Taste and adjust the seasoning as needed with crushed red pepper flakes, salt and pepper.

3. If not serving immediately, sprinkle a bit of lemon juice over the top, cover with plastic wrap touching the top of the guacamole, and store in the refrigerator for up to 2 days.

Louie's Note:
To remove the gills on a portobello, just pull off the stem then scrape out the brown stuff with a spoon. It only takes a few seconds, and it gives the mushroom a much nicer texture.

Chicken with Fresh Basil

Serves 4

2 tablespoons	soy sauce (or low-sodium soy sauce)
2 tablespoons	fish sauce* (preferably Squid brand)
1½ teaspoons	granulated sugar (or Splenda®)
3 tablespoons	canola oil
2 medium	yellow onions, chopped
3 cloves	garlic, minced
2 pounds	boneless, skinless chicken breasts, cut into bite-size chunks
1 (packed) cup	whole fresh basil leaves (or Thai basil*),
	plus extra for garnish
	salt and pepper, to taste
	crushed red pepper flakes, for garnish (optional)

1. Whisk together the soy sauce, fish sauce and sugar; set aside until needed.

2. Place a medium wok or sauté pan over medium-high heat; add the oil and heat through. Add the onions, tossing and stirring constantly (stir-frying), until somewhat tender, about 3 minutes. Add the garlic and stir-fry until the aroma is released, about 1 minute more.

3. Add the chicken to the wok, and stir-fry until golden brown, about 3 to 5 minutes.

4. Add the soy mixture and cook, stirring frequently, until the chicken is just cooked through, about 2 to 3 minutes more.

5. Remove the wok from the heat; stir in the fresh basil leaves, and toss to combine. Taste and season as needed with salt and pepper. Mound onto a serving platter and garnish with fresh basil sprigs and crushed red pepper flakes, if desired; serve immediately.

Available at your local Asian market

Louie's Note: If the basil leaves are very large, tear in half or thirds, depending upon the size. I love to eat this with some brown Thai Fried Rice (see recipe on page 143). Yum!

Grilled Tea-Marinated Duck Breasts with Apple Chutney

Serves 6

2 cups	hot water
4 single serving	tea bags
½ cup	granulated sugar (or Splenda®)
2 tablespoons	kosher salt
8 sprigs	fresh rosemary
2 medium	whole lemons, chopped
¼ cup	honey
6 (6 to 8-ounce)	boneless skinless duck breasts (or chicken breasts)
	Apple Chutney (recipe follows), as an accompaniment

1. Combine all of the ingredients except the duck and chutney in a small saucepot over medium heat; simmer until the sugar has fully dissolved. Cool completely, then add the duck breasts and marinate, refrigerated, overnight.

2. Preheat the grill to medium-high; clean and oil the grates to prevent sticking. Shake off the excess marinade, then grill the duck breasts for 4 minutes on each side. (Note: Duck breasts should always be served medium to medium-rare. If substituting chicken, cook until fully done or 165 degrees F internal temperature.) Serve the duck breasts topped with a nice spoonful of Apple Chutney and enjoy!

Louie's Note: Please try eating your duck cooked no longer than medium. Cooked further than medium, duck tastes like liver. If you want liver - go buy some - but don't do that to your duck! Just have chicken instead.

Apple Chutney

Serves 6

6 medium	Granny Smith apples, peeled, cored and finely diced
1 cup	light brown sugar (or Splenda® brown sugar)
½ cup	apple cider vinegar
1 teaspoon	kosher salt, or to taste
1 teaspoon	finely minced fresh ginger
¼ medium	red bell pepper, finely diced
¼ medium	yellow bell pepper, finely diced
	juice and zest of 2 lemons
1 tablespoon	chopped fresh parsley

1. Combine the apples, brown sugar, vinegar, salt and ginger in a medium saucepan over medium heat. Bring to a simmer.

2. Lower the heat, then add the peppers, lemon juice and zest. Simmer until the chutney has a nice, thick consistency, about 35 to 45 minutes. Do not over-cook, or it will turn into applesauce! Remove from the heat, and set aside to cool.

3. Once the chutney has cooled completely, add the chopped parsley. If not using immediately refrigerate, tightly covered, for up to 2 weeks.

Whole-Wheat Cilantro Pesto Tortilla Pizzas with Grilled Chicken and Pineapple

Serves 6

Pesto:

3 cups	fresh cilantro leaves (or basil leaves)
1 tablespoon	minced garlic
¼ cup	grated Parmesan cheese (1 ounce)
¼ cup	pine nuts, toasted
¼ cup	extra-virgin olive oil, or as needed
	salt and pepper, to taste

Pizza:

6 (8-inch)	whole-wheat tortillas
2 cups	shredded part skim mozzarella (8 ounces) (or low-fat mozzarella)
2 cups	diced grilled or rotisserie chicken
1 cup	fresh or unsweetened canned pineapple, diced
	crushed red pepper flakes, to taste

For the Pesto:

1. In a food processor or blender, combine the cilantro, garlic, cheese and pine nuts. With the motor running, slowly drizzle in the oil until creamy and emulsified. Taste, and season as needed with salt and pepper. If necessary, add a bit more oil to achieve the desired consistency.

For the Pizza:

2. Preheat the oven to 400 degrees F. Using tongs, place one tortilla at a time on top of a low-lit stovetop gas burner (or outdoor grill). Lightly char both sides until the tortillas feel slightly dry and hard. Transfer the tortillas to a baking sheet.

3. Spread 3 tablespoons of the pesto on each tortilla. Sprinkle with mozzarella, then top with diced chicken and pineapple.

4. Cook until golden brown and crispy, about 10 to 15 minutes. Sprinkle with crushed red pepper flakes, and serve hot.

Whole-Wheat Pizzas
Makes 2 (14-inch) pizzas

Dough:

1 tablespoon	granulated sugar (or Splenda®)
1 teaspoon	kosher salt
1½ cups	whole-wheat flour
2 cups	bread flour (hi-gluten flour)
1 large	egg
1 tablespoon	extra-virgin olive oil
1 tablespoon	active-dry yeast (1 packet)
1¼ cups	lukewarm water (110°F)

Pizza:

	cornmeal, as needed
2 cups	your favorite tomato sauce (or pizza sauce), divided
½ cup	grated Parmesan cheese (2 ounces), divided
3 cups	shredded mozzarella cheese (12 ounces) (or low-fat mozzarella cheese), divided
1 cup	your favorite topping(s),* divided

For the Dough:

1. Combine the sugar, salt, flours, egg and oil in an electric mixer with the dough hook attachment. Beat on medium-low speed for 3 minutes.

2. While the dough is mixing, dissolve the yeast in the warm water, and set aside until creamy. When ready, add the yeast mixture to the dough and continue mixing on medium speed until the dough forms a smooth ball, about 5 minutes more.

3. Use a dough cutter to divide the dough in half; place in 2 separate lightly oiled bowls. Cover each bowl with a kitchen towel or plastic wrap, and place in a warm area; let rise until doubled in size, about 1 hour.

For the Pizza:

4. Preheat the oven to 500 degrees F. Place a baking stone in the oven to preheat. On a floured table or board, roll and stretch each dough into a 14-inch circle.

5. Sprinkle cornmeal on your peel to prevent sticking. Place one dough on the peel, then ladle half of the sauce in the middle of the dough; spread the sauce, leaving a 1-inch border. Add half of each cheese and ½ cup of

your favorite topping(s), then slide the dough onto the hot baking stone. (Hot Tip: Hold the peel at an angle, and place the tip of the peel to the top of the stone; jerk and pull with the handle of the peel. The pizza should slide right off.)

6. Bake until crisp and golden brown, about 10 to 15 minutes. Repeat with the remaining ingredients to make a second pizza. Serve hot.

* *My Favorite Toppings: Crumbled turkey sausage, turkey pepperoni, turkey bacon, grilled chicken breast, goat cheese, sun-dried tomatoes and sautéed mushrooms.*

Louie's Note: Making pizza is a fun thing to do - you will feel like a pro! You can get a pizza-making set at a department store in the home and appliance section. Just make sure the stone comes with handles so it will be easy to remove from the oven.

Bruno's Wrap
Serves 2

½ cup	diced avocado (preferably Hass)
½ cup	sun-dried tomatoes (or diced fresh tomatoes)
4 slices	turkey bacon, cooked and crumbled
2 teaspoons	fresh lime juice
2 tablespoons	spicy honey mustard (or your favorite honey mustard)
	salt and pepper, to taste
2 (10-inch)	whole-wheat flour tortillas
8 ounces	grilled chicken strips, warmed
1 cup	fresh baby spinach (or your favorite lettuce)

1. Combine the avocados, tomatoes, bacon, lime juice and mustard in a small bowl; toss to combine. Adjust the seasoning as needed with salt and pepper.

2. Divide the avocado mixture evenly between the tortillas, leaving a 1-inch border around the edges. Top each with half the chicken and spinach. Roll like a burrito, and serve immediately.

Louie's Note: I like to slightly heat up my tortilla either on the stove over a gas flame or on the grill.

Thai Green Curry
with Chicken and Eggplant
Serves 1

2 tablespoons	canola oil
2 tablespoons	Thai green curry paste*
2 each	kaffir lime leaves*
1 (13.5-ounce) can	unsweetened coconut milk** (or light coconut milk)
1 (6-ounce)	boneless, skinless chicken breast, cut into bite-size pieces
¼ cup	canned straw mushrooms,* drained well
¼ cup	canned sliced bamboo shoots,* drained well
¼ cup	thinly sliced Japanese eggplant (or ½-inch cubes globe eggplant)
1 tablespoon	granulated sugar (or Splenda®)
1 tablespoon	fish sauce* (preferably Squid brand)
6 each	Thai basil leaves* (or Italian basil), plus extra sprig for garnish
¼ teaspoon	Asian chile powder* (or crushed red pepper flakes), or to taste
	Steamed Jasmine Rice (see recipe on page 144), as an accompaniment

1. Heat a medium wok or sauté pan over medium-high heat; add the oil and heat through. Stir in the curry paste and kaffir lime leaves and cook, stirring, until the aroma is released, about 2 minutes.

2. Slowly add the thin coconut milk to the paste, stirring constantly. Add the chicken, mushrooms, bamboo shoots, eggplant, sugar and fish sauce; simmer until the chicken and eggplant are fully cooked and tender, approximately 8 to 12 minutes.

3. Remove the curry from the heat, and stir in the basil leaves and all but one tablespoonful of the reserved coconut cream.

4. Serve the curry in a large Asian bowl garnished with the remaining tablespoon of coconut cream, a sprig of Thai basil, and a sprinkling of Asian chile powder (if desired). Serve immediately with steamed jasmine rice.

Available at your local Asian market

**Do not shake the can of coconut milk. Remove and reserve the thick cream from the top of the can – you will add it in at the end of the cooking time. Cook only with the thin coconut milk.*

Meat

Bistec Encebollado
(Steak and Onions)
Serves 6

½ cup	white vinegar (or fresh lemon juice)
1 tablespoon	minced garlic
¼ cup	Bruno's Dry Adobo Seasoning
	(or your favorite adobo), or to taste
3 pounds	beef tenderloin, sliced ½-inch thick
4 tablespoons	extra-virgin olive oil, divided
4 large	yellow onions, thinly sliced
3 tablespoons	chopped fresh parsley leaves

1. In a medium bowl, combine the vinegar, garlic and adobo; add the sliced beef, and toss to coat.

2. Heat a large sauté pan over medium heat; add 2 tablespoons of the oil and heat through. Add the onions to the hot pan and cook, stirring occasionally, until beginning to brown and caramelize, about 15 minutes. Transfer the onions to a plate, and tent with foil.

3. Place the same pan back over medium-high heat; add the remaining oil and heat through. Shake the excess marinade off the steaks, then place in the pan and brown on both sides. Add the onions back to the pan, and cook 3 to 5 minutes more. Serve on a large platter, family-style, and garnish with fresh parsley.

Louie's Note: Growing up, we used round steak which is a tougher piece of meat that takes a bit longer to cook. Filet of beef may be a bit pricey, but it's well worth it. Although the meat will cook to medium-well or well-done, it will be juicy and extremely tasty. Promise! Serve it with a small Cuban Salad (see recipe on page 50) and black beans with Spanish rice. OOhh yeah - and a glass of Sangria (see recipe on page 186)!

Smoked Barbecue Chipotle Beef Tenderloin

Serves 6 to 8

3 tablespoons	extra-virgin olive oil, divided
1 (5-pound)	beef tenderloin
1 to 2 tablespoons	Bruno's Smoked BBQ Chipotle Seasoning (or your favorite barbecue seasoning), or to taste yeast rolls, as an accompaniment Fresh Cranberry-Pecan Relish (recipe follows), as an accompaniment

1. Preheat the oven to 400 degrees F. Heat a medium, oven-proof sauté pan over medium-high heat; add 2 tablespoons of the oil and heat through.

2. Rub the tenderloin with the remaining oil, then season generously with barbecue seasoning; sear on all sides until crusty and golden brown, about 2 minutes. Transfer the pan to the oven, and roast to an internal temperature of 130 degrees F for medium-rare, about 20 to 25 minutes. (Or, cook to your desired degree of doneness.)

3. Remove the pan from the oven, and transfer the tenderloin to a cutting board; tent loosely with aluminum foil, and allow to rest for 10 minutes.

4. Use a very sharp slicing knife to carve the tenderloin into ¼-inch thick slices. Attractively arrange the sliced tenderloin on a platter, and serve with yeast rolls and Fresh Cranberry-Pecan Relish. Have your guests make little sandwiches. Delicious!

Fresh Cranberry-Pecan Relish
Serves 6 to 8

1 cup	fresh or thawed frozen cranberries
3 tablespoons	fresh orange juice
1 teaspoon	finely minced orange zest
1½ tablespoons	fresh lime juice (about 1 lime)
1 teaspoon	finely minced lime zest
½ cup	light brown sugar (or Splenda® brown sugar)
¼ to ½ teaspoon	kosher salt, or to taste
½ teaspoon	freshly ground black pepper, or to taste
2 tablespoons	chopped pecans, toasted
3 tablespoons	chopped fresh cilantro leaves
2 medium	roasted red bell peppers, peeled, seeded and diced

1. Combine the cranberries, orange juice and zest, lime juice and zest, brown sugar, salt and pepper in a food processor; pulse to combine, but do not puree.

2. Add the pecans and cilantro, and pulse 3 to 4 times. Add the roasted red peppers, and pulse 2 to 3 times more.

3. Place in the refrigerator for at least 1 hour (and up to 3 days) prior to serving. Serve well chilled.

Vaca Frita
(Crispy Fried Beef)
Serves 8

3 (1½-pound)	flank steaks
3 each	bay leaves
2 large	carrots, peeled and cut into 2-inch pieces
2 (14.5-ounce) cans	diced tomatoes (do not drain)
2 tablespoons	Bruno's Dry Adobo Seasoning (or your favorite adobo), or to taste
1½ quarts	fat-free low-sodium beef broth (6 cups)
2 cups	water
½ cup	extra-virgin olive oil, divided
2 large	yellow onions, thinly sliced
¼ cup	finely chopped fresh cilantro leaves
½ cup	fresh lime juice (about 6 limes)
	salt and pepper, to taste
	steamed white rice, as an accompaniment

1. In a medium stock pot, combine the steaks, bay leaves, carrots, tomatoes (and juices from tomatoes), adobo, broth and water over medium-high heat. Bring to a boil, then reduce the heat and simmer until the steaks are very tender, about 2½ to 3 hours.

2. Remove the steaks from the liquid, and set aside to cool; when cool enough to handle, shred with a fork. Place on a paper towel-lined platter, and tent with aluminum foil.

3. Place a large, hot sauté pan over high heat; add ¼ cup of the olive oil, and heat through. Add the shredded beef to the pan in an even layer, and cook both sides until brown and crispy. (You will probably need to cook the beef in batches to prevent over-crowding the pan.)

4. In a separate large sauté pan, add the remaining olive oil. Cook the onions over medium heat, stirring occasionally, until they are brown and caramelized, about 15 minutes.

5. Remove the pan from the heat, and drain off any excess oil. Add the crispy beef, cilantro and lime juice to the onions, then season to taste with salt and pepper; serve immediately with white rice.

Louie's Note: Vaca Frita is one of my childhood favorites. It is fantastic served over rice and beans!

Meatballs in Tomato Sauce

Serves 8

Meatballs:

3 pounds	ground chuck (or ground turkey or bison)
½ cup	grated manchego or Parmesan cheese
3 tablespoons	tomato paste
2 large	eggs, beaten
2 tablespoons	minced garlic
1 tablespoon	fresh thyme leaves, chopped
	salt and pepper, to taste
¼ cup	extra-virgin olive oil

Sauce:

4 (14.5-ounce) cans	diced tomatoes
½ cup	dry red wine
2 tablespoons	chopped fresh basil leaves, plus extra for garnish
1 tablespoon	finely chopped fresh rosemary
	salt and pepper, to taste

For the Meatballs:

1. In a medium bowl, gently mix all of the ingredients together except the oil. To test the seasoning, make a bite-size meatball and cook in a small pan (or in the microwave) until just cooked through. Taste, and adjust the seasoning as needed. Continue making test meatballs until the seasoning is just right. Once the seasoning is right, shape the mixture into 24 (2-ounce) meatballs.

2. Heat a large sauté pan over medium heat; add the oil and heat through. Add the meatballs and cook until browned on all sides.

For the Sauce:

3. Add the tomatoes, wine, basil and rosemary to the meatballs. Simmer gently until the meatballs are cooked through, about 20 minutes. Taste the sauce, and adjust the seasoning with salt and pepper as needed. Garnish with fresh basil, and serve hot.

Louie's Note: I'm a Bronx boy, so I love meatballs in tomato sauce served on bread as a meatball sub. But you can also serve them with your favorite pasta – for a healthier choice, make it whole-wheat pasta.

Peppercorn-Crusted Filets
with Molasses-Rum Glaze
Serves 8

Glaze:

2 tablespoons	extra-virgin olive oil
1 small	yellow onion, finely chopped
1 tablespoon	minced garlic
2 tablespoons	finely minced fresh ginger
¼ cup	dark rum
1 cup	molasses
2½ cups	bottled orange juice with pulp (such as Tropicana®)
	salt, to taste

Filets:

8 (8-ounce)	beef filets
	extra-virgin olive oil, as needed
1½ tablespoons	Bruno's Dry Adobo Seasoning (or your favorite adobo)
1 cup	coarsely ground black peppercorns, or as needed

For the Glaze:

1. Heat a small saucepan over medium-high heat; add the oil and heat through. Add the onion, garlic and ginger, and cook until the onions are tender, about 3 minutes. Add the rum, and reduce by half.

2. Add the molasses and orange juice, then taste and adjust the seasoning as needed with salt. Continue cooking the glaze until it reduces to about 1½ cups, about 20 minutes. Allow the glaze to cool to room temperature, then cover and refrigerate until needed.

For the Filets:

3. Preheat the grill to medium-high; clean and oil the grates to prevent sticking. Brush the filets with olive oil, and season with adobo; firmly press peppercorns onto both sides of each filet.

4. Grill until nicely seared on one side, about 4 to 5 minutes; flip the steaks over and cook to the desired doneness, about another 4 minutes for medium to medium-rare.

5. Remove the steaks from the grill and let rest for 3 to 4 minutes; drizzle Molasses-Rum Glaze over the steaks, and serve immediately.

Hoisin Lime Ribs

Serves 6

Hoisin Lime BBQ Sauce:

2 (2-inch) pieces	fresh ginger, peeled and chopped
4 cloves	garlic, peeled
¾ cup	red wine vinegar
½ cup	soy sauce (or low-sodium soy sauce)
½ cup	ketchup (or reduced-sugar ketchup)
1 small bunch	fresh cilantro
½ cup	fresh lime juice (about 6 limes)
	zest of 2 limes
⅓ cup	dark brown sugar (or Splenda® brown sugar)
¼ cup	hoisin sauce
1 tablespoon	crushed red pepper flakes, or to taste

Ribs:

¼ cup	ground allspice
2 tablespoons	kosher salt
2 tablespoons	freshly ground black pepper
1 tablespoon	ground coriander
2 racks	baby back ribs
1 cup	water or beer

For the Hoisin Lime BBQ Sauce:

1. Combine all of the Hoisin Lime BBQ Sauce ingredients in a blender; mix until smooth, and set aside until needed.

For the Ribs:

2. Preheat the oven to 375 degrees F. In a small mixing bowl, whisk together the allspice, salt, pepper and coriander. Season both sides of the ribs generously with the rub.

3. Pour the water or beer into a large roasting pan; place the dry-rubbed ribs in the pan. Seal tightly with aluminum foil, and bake until tender, about 2½ hours.

4. Remove the foil, and coat the ribs liberally with Hoisin Lime BBQ Sauce. Bake, uncovered, until the sauce thickens and glazes the ribs, about 10 to 15 minutes. Remove from the oven and cool slightly before serving.

Louie's Note: These ribs will cut like butter, and then you will want to slap someone - but not your mama. After you take a bite - Wow!

Smoked BBQ Chipotle Guava Ribs

Serves 8

Guava BBQ Sauce:

1 (9-ounce) jar	guava jelly
2 each	chipotle peppers in adobo sauce*
½ cup	ketchup (or reduced-sugar ketchup)
½ cup	dark corn syrup
½ cup	molasses
⅓ cup	red wine vinegar
2 tablespoons	yellow mustard
1 tablespoon	ground cumin
1 tablespoon	minced garlic
1 cup	dry white wine
	salt and pepper, to taste

Ribs:

4 racks	baby back ribs
½ cup	Bruno's Dry Adobo Seasoning (or your favorite adobo)
1 cup	water or beer

For the Guava BBQ Sauce:

1. Combine all of the Guava BBQ Sauce ingredients in a small saucepan; simmer over medium heat until reduced by half, about 45 minutes to an hour. Remove from the heat, and set aside to cool. If not using immediately, cool completely then store, tightly covered, in the refrigerator for up to 5 days.

For the Ribs:

2. Preheat the oven to 375 degrees F. Season both sides of the ribs with adobo. Pour the water or beer into a large roasting pan; place the dry-rubbed ribs in the pan. Seal tightly with aluminum foil, and bake until tender, about 2½ hours.

3. Remove the foil, and coat the ribs liberally with Guava BBQ Sauce. Bake, uncovered, until the sauce thickens and glazes the ribs, about 10 to 15 minutes. Remove from the oven and cool slightly before serving.

Purchase 1 can of chipotles in adobo, and spoon out 2 little peppers. Add a little bit of the adobo sauce for increased flavor and spice! Refrigerate the remainder, and save for another use.

Louie's Note: If you are worried about the sugar in the Guava BBQ Sauce, try the Guilt-Free Chipotle BBQ Sauce instead!

Guilt–Free Chipotle BBQ Sauce

Makes 3 cups

1 cup	brown sugar Splenda®
½ cup	honey
½ cup	reduced-sugar ketchup
2 each	chipotle peppers in adobo sauce*
⅓ cup	red wine vinegar
2 tablespoons	yellow mustard
1 tablespoon	ground cumin
1 tablespoon	minced garlic
1 cup	dry white wine
	salt and pepper, to taste

1. Combine all of the ingredients in a medium saucepan over medium heat; reduce the heat to a simmer and cook until reduced by half, about 25 to 30 minutes. Taste, and adjust the seasoning as needed with salt and pepper.

2. If not using immediately, cool completely then store, tightly covered, in the refrigerator for up to 5 days.

Purchase 1 can of chipotles in adobo, and spoon out 2 little peppers. Add a little bit of the adobo sauce for increased flavor and spice! Refrigerate the remainder, and save for another use.

Louie's Note: Try this on grilled chicken or a juicy grilled burger.

Sandwich Cubano

(Cuban Sandwich)

Serves 2

1 (12-inch) loaf	Cuban bread (recipe follows - or substitute French bread or whole-grain French bread)
3 tablespoons	yellow mustard
8 each	dill pickle slices
¼ pound	Swiss cheese (or low-fat mozzarella), thinly sliced
¼ pound	ham (or smoked turkey), thinly sliced
¼ pound	roasted pork loin, thinly sliced
2 tablespoons	Garlic and Cilantro Mojo (see recipe on page 35), or melted butter

1. Split the bread in half lengthwise. Spread mustard on both sides of the bread. On one side of the bread, make a layer of pickles, cheese, ham and pork loin; top with the other side of the bread loaf.

2. Preheat a sandwich press (or panini maker) to 350 degrees F. Brush the bottom and top of the sandwich with the Garlic and Cilantro Mojo. Place the sandwich in the press until crisp and golden brown, about 5 to 8 minutes.

3. Cut the sandwich in half at a diagonal, and serve hot.

Pan Cubano
(Cuban Bread)
Makes 2 loaves

2 (¼-ounce) packets	active-dry yeast (½ ounce)
1 tablespoon	granulated sugar
2 cups	warm water (110 degrees F)
6 cups	all-purpose flour
1 tablespoon	kosher salt
4 tablespoons	melted shortening or butter (2 ounces), divided (see Louie's Note)

1. Dissolve the yeast and sugar in the warm water. Stir well, and set aside until creamy and foamy, about 10 minutes.

2. Combine the flour and salt in a five-quart mixer with the dough hook attachment; mix well. Add 3 tablespoons of the melted shortening, and mix on low speed for 1 minute. Add the yeast mixture, and beat on medium speed until the dough is smooth and velvety, about 5 minutes.

3. Grease a large mixing bowl with the remaining shortening. Place the dough in the bowl, and flip it over to make sure the dough is covered in shortening on top and bottom. Cover the bowl with a dry towel and then with plastic wrap. Place in a warm area in your kitchen, and let it rise until doubled in size, about 1 hour.

4. Once the dough has doubled, turn it out onto a lightly floured work surface. Using a dough cutter, divide the dough into two equal pieces. Shape each loaf by stretching and rolling the dough into a long sausage-like shape, about 12 inches long and 3 inches in diameter.

5. Set the loaves about three inches apart on a parchment paper-lined baking sheet. Cover the loaves lightly with a kitchen towel, and allow to rise for about 15 minutes. Using a very sharp knife, make three short slashes on each loaf, then gently brush with water. Preheat the oven to 400 degrees F.

6. Place a pan of boiling water in the bottom of the oven to create steam. Bake the loaves until golden brown, about 35 to 45 minutes. Allow to cool before slicing – if you can make yourself wait!

Louie's Note: For best results, use shortening – just make sure that it is a shortening that contains zero trans fats.

Avocado-Lime Crema
Makes about 2½ cups

¼ cup	fresh lime juice (about 3 limes)
1½ cups	sour cream (or light sour cream)
2 medium	ripe but firm avocados (preferable Hass), pitted, peeled and diced
½ cup	fresh cilantro leaves, chopped
	salt and pepper, to taste
	hot sauce (such as Tabasco®), to taste

1. Combine all of the ingredients in a blender; mix until smooth. Taste and adjust the seasoning as needed with salt, pepper and hot sauce.

2. Chill, tightly covered with plastic wrap, for one hour before serving. (Make up to one day in advance.)

Louie's Note: This sauce is great on Empanadas (see recipe on page 14). I also enjoy it on a nice piece of grilled steak…Oh, yeah!

Sofrito

Makes about 2 cups

1 small head	garlic (about 10 cloves)
1 medium	green bell pepper (stem, ribs and seeds removed), chopped
1 medium	red bell pepper (stem, ribs and seeds removed), chopped
1 small bunch	fresh cilantro
1 tablespoon	Bruno's Dry Adobo Seasoning (or your favorite adobo)
1 medium	yellow onion, diced
½ teaspoon	dried oregano
½ cup	extra-virgin olive oil

1. Combine all of the ingredients except the oil in a blender; with the motor running, slowly drizzle in the oil until creamy and emulsified.

2. Place the mixture in a medium sauté pan over medium-high heat; cook, stirring, until slightly thickened and fragrant, about 3 to 5 minutes.

3. Cool completely then store, tightly covered, in the refrigerator for up to 3 weeks (or freeze for up to 3 months).

Louie's Note: My mom uses Sofrito to spice up her soups and rice dishes. It really can be used to flavor anything- just add a couple of spoonfuls to whatever you are cooking, and you get instant flavor. I like to heat up some of my Sofrito and serve it over grilled lean cuts of beef or sautéed chicken breasts. I even use it as a sauce for grilled fish, but don't tell my mom about this!

Fish & Seafood

Grilled Miso–Marinated Sea Bass

Serves 6

¼ cup	red miso*
¼ cup	mirin*
1 tablespoon	granulated sugar (or Splenda®)
2 tablespoons	unseasoned rice vinegar*
2 tablespoons	finely minced fresh ginger
6 (6-ounce)	sea bass fillets
	salt and pepper, to taste

1. In a medium bowl, whisk together the miso, mirin, sugar, vinegar and ginger. Coat the fillets with the marinade on both sides, then place in the refrigerator and marinate for 4 hours.

2. Preheat the grill to medium. Clean and oil the grates to prevent sticking. Remove any excess marinade, and season the fillets lightly with salt and pepper.

3. Grill the fillets until just cooked through, about 5 minutes per side. Remove from the grill, and serve hot.

Available at your local Asian market.

Louie's Note: Sea bass is a succulent, flaky fish with an amazing buttery taste. Try this dish with Thai Fried Rice (see recipe on page 143).

Grilled Salmon with Sake–Soy–Tamarind Glaze
Serves 4

Glaze:

2 tablespoons	canola oil
2 tablespoons	minced shallots
2 cloves	garlic, minced
½ cup	sake (or dry white wine)
2 (6 to 8-inch) pieces	fresh ginger
1 cup	soy sauce
½ cup	honey
1 tablespoon	Knorr® Tamarind Soup Base*

Salmon:

4 (8-ounce)	salmon fillets
2 tablespoons	canola oil
	salt and pepper, to taste

For the Glaze:

1. Heat a small sauté pan over medium-high heat; add the oil and heat through. Stir in the shallots, and cook until soft. Add the garlic and cook until fragrant, about 1 minute more.

2. Add the sake, being careful to avoid any flare-ups that may occur. Stir vigorously to remove any stuck bits from the bottom of the pan.

3. Grate the pieces of ginger on the large holes of a box grater (also known as a cheese grater). You don't even have to peel the ginger. Gather up the grated ginger bits, and squeeze the juice into a small bowl; measure out 2 tablespoonfuls, and add to the hot pan. Discard the pulp after squeezing out the juice.

4. Stir in the soy sauce, honey and tamarind soup base, and bring to a boil; immediately reduce the heat to medium to medium-low. Simmer until reduced by half. (Watch the glaze carefully, because it could easily boil over or burn!) Remove from the heat, and set aside until needed.

For the Salmon:

5. Gently rub the fillets with oil, then season with salt and pepper. Preheat the grill to medium-high; clean and oil the grates to prevent sticking.

6. Place the fillets onto the grill skin-side down – that is, the side where the skin used to be. After about 3 minutes, carefully flip the fish fillets over, and brush thickly with glaze; cook until the fish is just cooked through, about 3 minutes more. With a metal spatula, gently remove the fish from the grill, and serve immediately.

Available at your local Asian market.

Louie's Note: If you would like to add a little kick to your glaze, add ¾ teaspoon crushed red pepper flakes to the pan while you are sautéing the shallots. If you want to make sure your fish is done, test with an instant-read thermometer. For medium-rare, cook to an internal temperature of 120 degrees F. For medium to medium-well, cook to 130 to 135 degrees F.

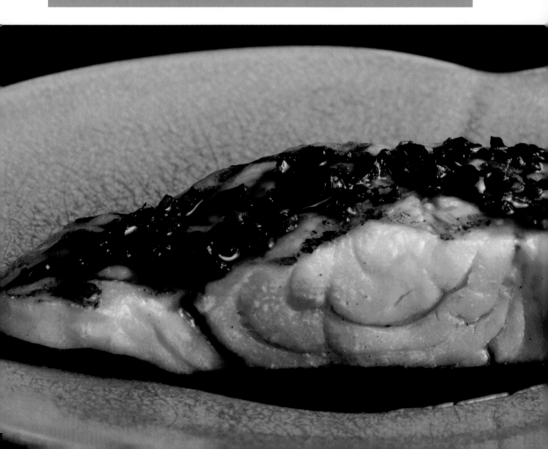

Shrimp with Spicy Chili Sauce
Serves 6

¾ cup	Asian chili garlic sauce*
1 tablespoon	finely minced fresh ginger
¼ cup	ketchup (or reduced-sugar ketchup)
1 tablespoon	soy sauce (or low-sodium soy sauce)
1½ tablespoons	brown sugar (or Splenda® brown sugar)
1½ cups	low-sodium, non-fat chicken broth
	juice of 2 limes
¼ cup	water
2 tablespoons	cornstarch
2 pounds	jumbo shrimp (16/20 count), peeled and deveined, tails off
½ cup	fresh cilantro leaves, chopped
3 to 4 each	green onions, green tops only, thinly sliced at a diagonal
	salt and pepper, to taste

1. Combine the Asian chili garlic sauce, ginger, ketchup, soy sauce, brown sugar, broth and lime juice in a large sauté pan over medium heat; simmer for 8 to 10 minutes.

2. In a small bowl, whisk together the water and cornstarch. Bring the chili sauce mixture to a boil, then whisk in the cornstarch mixture; boil for 1 minute.

3. Reduce the heat to a simmer, and add the shrimp; cook until pink and just cooked through, about 3 to 5 minutes. The sauce should be thick and glossy.

4. Remove the pan from the heat, and stir in the cilantro and green onions. Taste, and adjust the seasoning as needed with salt and pepper; serve immediately.

*Available at your local Asian market.

Louie's Note: This dish is unbelievable on brown Thai Fried Rice (see recipe on page 143). Substitute chicken for the shrimp if you like – delicious!

Sambal

Makes 2 cups

¾ cup	shallots, chopped
1 whole head	fresh garlic (peel each clove)
½ cup	chopped fresh lemongrass*
1½ teaspoons	shrimp paste**
2 tablespoons	water
¼ cup	canola oil
½ cup	Asian chili garlic sauce**
1 tablespoon	granulated sugar (or Splenda®)

1. Combine the shallots, garlic, lemongrass, shrimp paste and water in a blender; pulverize until smooth.

2. Heat a medium wok or sauté pan over medium heat; add the oil and heat through. Add the lemongrass mixture to the wok and cook, tossing and stirring constantly (stir-frying) until the aroma is released, about 5 to 8 minutes.

3. Add the chili garlic sauce and sugar, and stir-fry until the oil floats on top of the mixture. Remove from the heat, and set aside to cool. When completely cool store, refrigerated, in an airtight container for up to 1 month.

Use only the tender pale green tips of the lemongrass stalk. Remove and discard the tough outer leaves.

**Available at your local Asian market.*

Rosemary Shrimp Pasta
Serves 6

1 pound	bow tie pasta (or your favorite whole-wheat pasta)
½ cup	extra-virgin olive oil
¼ cup	fresh rosemary needles
2 cloves	garlic, minced
1 teaspoon	crushed red pepper flakes, or to taste
1 pound	large shrimp (21/25 count), peeled and deveined, tails off
	juice of 1 lemon
½ cup	finely grated Parmesan cheese (2 ounces)
	salt and pepper, to taste

1. Cook the pasta to al dente (tender but with a firm bite); drain, and set aside.

2. Combine the oil and rosemary in a blender, and mix on high speed until the rosemary is completely pulverized, about 3 minutes. Set aside.

3. Place a large sauté pan over medium heat; add 2 tablespoons of the rosemary oil and heat through. Add the garlic and crushed red pepper flakes, and cook until fragrant, about 30 seconds. Add the shrimp, and sauté until pink and just cooked through, about 3 minutes more.

4. Add the pasta, lemon juice and remaining rosemary oil to the sauté pan, and toss with the shrimp mixture. Cook, stirring frequently, until warmed through.

5. Remove the pan from the heat, and add the cheese; toss to combine. Taste, and adjust the seasoning as needed with salt and pepper. Serve hot or at room temperature.

Louie's Note: This recipe is ideal for a ladies' luncheon - or just for a quick healthful meal. You can even pack it in a picnic, as it can be served at room temperature.

Macadamia Nut–Crusted Grouper with Tropical Fruit Salsa
Serves 6

6 (6-ounce)	grouper fillets (or other flaky white fish fillets)
	salt and cayenne pepper, to taste
3 large	eggs, beaten
1 cup	whole milk (or 2% milk)
1 cup	macadamia nuts
4 cups	corn flakes, crushed, divided
1½ cups	all-purpose flour (or oat flour)
	Tropical Fruit Salsa (recipe follows), as an accompaniment

1. Season the fish fillets with salt and cayenne on both sides; set aside. Whisk together the eggs and milk; set aside.

2. In a food processor, grind the macadamia nuts and 1 cup of the corn flakes to fine crumbs, about 2 minutes. Add the mixture to the remaining 3 cups of crushed cornflakes. Preheat the oven to 400 degrees F.

3. Set up a breading procedure as follows: Place the flour, egg mixture and corn flake mixture in separate shallow dishes. Then, dip each fish fillet in the flour, then in the egg mixture, then in the corn flake mixture; coat well.

4. Place the crusted fish on a non-stick (or lightly oiled) baking sheet, and bake until just cooked through, about 12 to 15 minutes. Transfer the fish to a large serving platter; serve hot with Tropical Fruit Salsa.

Tropical Fruit Salsa:

1 medium	papaya, peeled and seeded, finely diced
1 medium	mango, peeled and pitted, finely diced
2 medium	kiwi fruits, peeled and finely diced
	juice of 1 lime
1½ tablespoons	finely chopped fresh cilantro leaves
2 tablespoons	finely diced red onions
2 tablespoons	finely diced red bell pepper

In a medium bowl, toss together all of the ingredients. If not serving immediately, store in an airtight container in the refrigerator for up to 2 days.

Louie's Note: A little Caribbean Mojo (see recipe on page 116) drizzled around the plate or over the crusted fish would be a nice touch.

Caribbean Mojo

Makes 2½ cups

2 cloves	garlic, minced
2 tablespoons	extra-virgin olive oil
	juice of 3 limes
	juice of 3 oranges
2 cups	diced fresh ripe papaya (or mango or pineapple)
1 teaspoon	crushed red pepper flakes, or to taste
1 teaspoon	granulated sugar (or Splenda®), or to taste
	salt and pepper, to taste
2 tablespoons	chopped fresh cilantro leaves

1. Combine the garlic and olive oil in a medium sauté pan over medium heat; cook just until the aroma is released, about 1 minute.

2. Add the citrus juices, fruit, crushed red pepper flakes, sugar, salt and pepper, and simmer for about 10 minutes. Taste, and adjust the seasoning as needed with crushed red pepper flakes, sugar, salt and pepper.

3. Transfer the mojo to a clean bowl, and set aside to cool completely. When completely cool, add the cilantro. Serve chilled or at room temperature.

Louie's Note: If your fruit is fully ripened and very sweet, then the sugar may not be necessary. If the fruit is seriously under-ripe, additional sugar may be needed to balance the flavors. Try this mojo with flaky white fish, chicken or pork. It'll transport you to the islands!

Adobo Fried Shrimp Soft Tacos with Smoked BBQ Chipotle Coleslaw

Serves 6

Coleslaw:

½ cup	sour cream (or light sour cream)
2 tablespoons	mayonnaise (or light mayonnaise)
	juice of 2 limes
1 (16-ounce) package	coleslaw mix
¼ cup	fresh cilantro leaves, chopped
1 small bunch	green onions, green tops only, thinly sliced
1 tablespoon	Bruno's Smoked BBQ Chipotle Seasoning (or your favorite barbecue seasoning), or to taste

Shrimp:

	canola oil, for frying
2 cups	all-purpose flour (or whole-wheat flour)
1 cup	cornmeal
1 pound medium	shrimp (26/30 count), peeled and deveined
2 tablespoons	Bruno's Dry Adobo Seasoning (or your favorite adobo), or to taste
6 (8-inch)	flour tortillas (or whole-wheat tortillas)

For the Coleslaw:

1. In medium bowl, combine all of the ingredients. Mix well, then taste and adjust the seasoning as needed. Place in the refrigerator for about an hour.

For the Shrimp:

2. Heat the oil in a large saucepan (or deep fryer) to 375 degrees F.

3. In a medium bowl, combine the flour and cornmeal; set aside. Season the shrimp with the adobo. Dredge the seasoned shrimp in the cornmeal mixture, then add to the hot oil one at a time. Fry until golden brown, about 3 minutes. Drain on paper towels. (If you prefer, grill the shrimp for a lighter dish.)

4. Heat a medium sauté pan over medium-high heat; add a tortilla, and heat for about 30 seconds on each side.

5. Spoon about 2 tablespoons of slaw in the center of the tortilla; place 4 or 5 fried shrimp on top and fold like a taco. Repeat with the remaining ingredients. Serve hot or at room temperature.

Pad Thai with Shrimp
Serves 6

Pad Thai Sauce:

¼ cup	fish sauce* (preferably Squid brand)
½ cup	white vinegar
1 tablespoon	Knorr® Tamarind Soup Base*
½ cup	granulated sugar (or Splenda®), or to taste

Pad Thai:

12 ounces	medium rice stick noodles*
1 (12-ounce) block	extra-firm tofu*
5 tablespoons	canola oil, divided
4 cloves	garlic, minced
2 medium	shallots, chopped
1½ pounds large	shrimp (21/25 count), peeled and deveined
¼ cup	chopped preserved radishes* (optional)
1 teaspoon	crushed red pepper flakes, or to taste
½ cup	water
1 tablespoon	paprika
1 cup	fresh bean sprouts, washed well, for garnish
4 to 6	green onions, green tops only, very thinly sliced, for garnish
½ cup	finely chopped roasted peanuts, for garnish
1 medium	lime, cut into wedges, for garnish

For the Pad Thai Sauce:

1. In a small saucepan, combine the fish sauce, vinegar, tamarind soup base and sugar. Cook over medium-high heat until the sugar dissolves and the mixture thickens, about 10 to 12 minutes.

For the Pad Thai:

2. Soak the dried rice noodles in lukewarm water until somewhat tender but still firm to the touch, about 1 hour; drain well and set aside.

3. Cut the tofu into 1-inch cubes; heat a large wok or sauté pan over high heat; add 2 tablespoons of the oil and heat through. Add the tofu and stir-fry until golden brown; set aside.

4. Place the wok back over medium-high heat until it is smoking hot. Add the remaining 3 tablespoons of oil, then toss in the garlic, shallots, shrimp, radishes and crushed red pepper flakes; stir-fry for 30 seconds.

5. Add the drained noodles and ¼ cup water to the wok, stirring and tossing quickly to separate the strands. Pour in the Pad Thai Sauce and paprika, tossing well to coat the noodles and prevent them from sticking. Stir-fry until the noodles are tender and the sauce has thickened slightly, about 4 to 5 minutes.

6. Add the cooked tofu and stir-fry for another 3 to 4 minutes, tossing to combine and warm the tofu through. Garnish with bean sprouts, green onions, chopped peanuts and lime wedges. Serve immediately.

Available at your local Asian market.

Sesame Seared Tuna
with Edamame "Hummus"
Serves 4

Hummus:

2 cups	shelled edamame* (Japanese green soybeans)
2 tablespoons	red miso*
¼ cup	fresh lemon juice (about 1½ lemons)
1 tablespoon	Asian chile oil*
¼ teaspoon	kosher salt, or to taste
⅛ teaspoon	freshly ground black pepper, or to taste
¼ cup	chicken broth, or as needed to thin

Tuna:

1½ tablespoons	prepared wasabi*
4 (6-ounce)	fresh sashimi-grade Ahi tuna steaks (about 1-inch thick)
	salt and pepper, to taste
½ cup	black sesame seeds*
½ cup	white sesame seeds
2 tablespoons	canola oil, or as needed
20 each	Sesame Pita Chips (see recipe on page 17), as an accompaniment
2 each	green onions, green tops only, thinly sliced, for garnish

For the Hummus:

1. Cook the edamame in boiling salted water until tender, about 5 to 8 minutes. Drain well, then place in a food processor with the miso, lemon juice, chile oil, salt and pepper; pulse to combine. With the motor running, drizzle the broth through the feed tube and process until the mixture is somewhat smooth. Taste, and adjust the seasoning as needed with salt and pepper.

For the Tuna:

2. Spread wasabi on both sides of each tuna steak, then season with salt and pepper. Mix the black and white sesame seeds together, and place on a plate. Press each tuna steak into the sesame seeds on both sides to create a crust.

3. Heat a large, non-stick sauté pan over high heat; add the oil and heat through. Sear each tuna steak on both sides until golden brown, about 30 seconds to 1 minute. (You may need to wipe out the pan with paper towel and add new oil between batches.) If you prefer your fish cooked longer, transfer to a 350 degree F oven until the desired degree of doneness is achieved, about 3 to 5 minutes longer.

4. Slice the tuna steaks crosswise into ¼-inch thick slices, and fan out on each dinner plate. Serve with a nice spoonful of Edamame Hummus and 5 Sesame Pita Chips. Garnish with green onions and serve at room temperature.

*Available at your local Asian market

Escabèche de Pescado

(Marinated Fish)

Serves 4

Marinade:

1 cup	extra-virgin olive oil
½ cup	white vinegar
¼ cup	black peppercorns, cracked
1 teaspoon	kosher salt
2 each	bay leaves
1 large	yellow onion, thinly sliced
1 cup	small olives, pitted
¼ cup	small capers
¼ cup	fresh parsley leaves, chopped

Fish:

2 pounds	flaky white fish (such as snapper), cut into 4-ounce fillets
2 tablespoons	fresh lemon juice
2 cloves	garlic, minced
1 tablespoon	Bruno's Dry Adobo Seasoning (or your favorite adobo), or to taste
2 cups	all-purpose flour (or oat flour)
½ cup	extra-virgin olive oil

For the Marinade:

1. Combine the marinade ingredients in a medium saucepot over medium heat; simmer, stirring occasionally, for 45 minutes. Cool to room temperature, then place in a glass bowl to chill.

For the Fish:

2. Season the fish with lemon juice, garlic and adobo, then dredge in the flour. Heat a large sauté pan over medium heat; add the oil and heat through. Fry the fish until golden brown, about 2 to 3 minutes per side. (The fish may be slightly under-cooked, but it will finish "cooking" in the marinade.) Drain on paper towels.

3. Pour half of the marinade into a large glass casserole dish; place the fish on top. Pour the remaining marinade over the fish. Cover, and marinate in the refrigerator for at least 4 hours and up to overnight; serve cold.

Garlic Shrimp

Serves 4

3 to 4 tablespoons	extra-virgin olive oil
1 tablespoon	minced garlic
2 each	bay leaves
1 teaspoon	crushed red pepper flakes, or to taste
2 pounds	jumbo shrimp (16/20 count), peeled and deveined, tails on
	salt and pepper, to taste
2 tablespoons	chopped fresh parsley leaves, for garnish

1. Heat a large sauté pan over medium-high heat; add the oil and heat through.

2. Add the garlic, bay leaves and red pepper flakes, and cook, stirring constantly, until fragrant, about 30 seconds. Do not burn the garlic!

3. Add the shrimp, and season generously with salt and pepper. Sauté until the shrimp are pink and just cooked through, about 3 minutes. Do not over-cook, or the shrimp will be rubbery! Taste, and adjust the seasoning as needed with salt and pepper.

4. Transfer the shrimp to a serving dish, and garnish with fresh parsley. Serve hot or at room temperature.

Louie's Note: When you ask for 16/20 count shrimp at the market, that means the size and the number you are getting per pound. So you would get 16 to 20 shrimp per pound in 16/20 count shrimp.

Rosemary–Garlic Shrimp

Serves 4

2 tablespoons	extra-virgin olive oil
3 cloves	garlic, minced
2 pounds	jumbo shrimp (16/20 count), peeled and deveined, tails on
	salt and pepper, to taste
½ cup	dry white wine
½ cup	Rosemary Butter (recipe follows)
1 loaf	French bread (or whole-grain French bread),
	as an accompaniment

1. Heat a large sauté pan over high heat; add the oil and heat through. Add the garlic and cook until fragrant, about 30 seconds. Add the shrimp and sauté 2 minutes more. Season to taste with salt and pepper.

2. Add the wine and cook until reduced by half, about 2 minutes.

3. Add the Rosemary Butter, and toss to combine. When the shrimp are just cooked through, taste and season with salt and pepper as needed. Remove the shrimp from the heat, and serve hot with crusty French bread for dipping in the sauce.

Rosemary Butter

Makes 1 pound

1 pound	unsalted butter (or healthy butter alternative such as Smart Balance® Buttery Spread), brought to room temperature
	zest and juice of 2 lemons
2 tablespoons	minced fresh rosemary
2 cloves	garlic, minced
	salt and pepper, to taste

1. Combine all of the ingredients in an electric mixer; beat with the paddle attachment until thoroughly combined.

2. Transfer to a sheet of parchment paper or plastic wrap, and shape into a log. Or, place in an airtight container and refrigerate until ready to use.

3. Refrigerate for up to 2 weeks, or freeze for up to 3 months.

Louie's Note: This is incredible on seafood!! And believe it or not, it's also great on a nice piece of lean grilled beef.

Spicy Mexican Shrimp Ceviche

Serves 6

1 pound	large shrimp (21/25 count), peeled and deveined, tails off
½ cup	fresh lime juice (about 6 limes)
½ cup	ketchup (or reduced-sugar ketchup)
1 tablespoon	hot sauce (such as Tabasco®), or to taste
2 tablespoons	white vinegar
½ small	red onion, very finely diced
1 cup	peeled, seeded and finely diced cucumber
2 small	ripe avocados (preferably Hass), pitted, peeled and diced
4 each	green onions, green tops only, thinly sliced
⅓ cup	fresh cilantro leaves, finely chopped
	salt and pepper, to taste

1. Bring a medium saucepan of salted water to a boil; add the shrimp, and immediately remove from the heat. Stir the shrimp until they are pink, opaque and just barely cooked through, about 3 to 5 minutes. (Do not over-cook, because the shrimp will continue to "cook" in the citrus marinade. You don't want rubbery shrimp!) Transfer the shrimp to a large glass or stainless steel bowl to cool completely.

2. Pour the lime juice over the shrimp, and toss to coat; cover and refrigerate for 30 to 45 minutes.

3. Whisk together the ketchup, hot sauce and vinegar; pour over the shrimp and lime juice, and toss to coat. Add the red onions, cucumbers, avocados, green onions and cilantro, and gently toss together. Taste, and adjust the seasoning with salt and pepper. Cover and refrigerate for at least 30 minutes and up to 4 hours. Serve with tortilla chips or saltines.

Paella
Serves 8 to 12

4 tablespoons	extra-virgin olive oil, divided
1 (3½ to 4-pound)	chicken, cut into eight pieces (or equivalent boneless, skinless chicken breasts)
2 tablespoons	Bruno's Dry Adobo Seasoning, (or your favorite adobo), or to taste
1 medium	yellow onion, finely diced
1 tablespoon	minced garlic
2 tablespoons	small capers
½ cup	pitted green olives
4 ounces	fresh chorizo (see recipe on page 61 or purchase)
3 cups	arborio rice (or brown rice)
2 teaspoons	saffron, chopped
	salt and pepper, to taste
1½ quarts	fat-free low-sodium chicken broth (6 cups)
1 pound	large shrimp (21/25 count), peeled and deveined, tails off
15 each	mussels, purged and cleaned (optional)
15 each	littleneck clams, purged and cleaned (optional)
1 pound	jumbo lump crabmeat
½ cup	frozen green peas, thawed
1 (6-ounce) jar	roasted red peppers, drained and thinly sliced
¼ cup	fresh cilantro leaves, chopped

1. Rub 1 tablespoon of olive oil on the chicken, then season with adobo. Place in the refrigerator for at least 1 hour and up to overnight.

2. Place a paella pan (or a deep, wide saucepot) over medium-high heat; add the remaining olive oil and heat through. Sear the chicken on all sides until dark golden brown, about 5 minutes. Transfer the chicken to a plate, and tent with foil. Do not wipe out the pan.

3. Place the same pan back over medium-high heat; add the onions, garlic, capers and olives, and sauté for about 3 minutes. Add the chorizo and cook 3 minutes more. Add the rice and saffron, and stir to mix; season to taste with salt and pepper. Add the broth, stirring to combine. Arrange the seared chicken pieces on top of the rice.

4. Cook, uncovered, over medium heat until the broth has evaporated, about 25 to 30 minutes; do not stir while cooking.

5. Add the shrimp, mussels and clams, and cover the pan. Once the mussels and clams have fully opened and the shrimp are fully cooked, add the crabmeat, peas and roasted red peppers. Discard any unopened mussels or clams. Cover 1 minute more to warm the crabmeat, peas and peppers; uncover, garnish with fresh cilantro, and serve hot.

Louie's Note: Paella is the perfect one-dish meal, and it makes a beautiful buffet presentation. Serve with a Cuban Salad (see recipe on page 50) and a pitcher of Sangria (see recipe on page 186).

Grilled Banana Leaf–Wrapped Fish with Red Curry Sauce

Serves 6

Sauce:

1 large	yellow onion, coarsely chopped
2 cloves	garlic, coarsely chopped
½ (packed) cup	fresh cilantro leaves, plus extra for garnish
4 whole	kaffir lime leaves,* center ribs removed, coarsely chopped
3 tablespoons	canola oil
2 tablespoons	Thai red curry paste,* or to taste
1 tablespoon	paprika
1 (13.5-ounce) can	unsweetened coconut milk* (or light coconut milk) (shake can well before opening)
1 tablespoon	granulated sugar (or Splenda®), or to taste
2 tablespoons	fish sauce* (preferably Squid brand), or to taste

Fish:

6 (6 to 8-ounce)	white fish fillets (such as grouper or snapper)
2 tablespoons	fresh lemon juice
	salt and pepper, to taste
	canola oil, as needed
6 each	banana leaves* (fresh or frozen), trimmed to fit fillet size
	fresh cilantro leaves, for garnish
	Steamed Jasmine Rice (see recipe on page 144), as an accompaniment

For the Sauce:

1. Combine the onions, garlic, cilantro and kaffir lime leaves in a food processor; pulse to form a paste.

2. Heat a small saucepan over medium-high heat; add the oil, and heat through. Sauté the onion mixture until the aroma is released, about 4 to 5 minutes. Add the red curry paste and paprika, and cook 3 minutes more.

3. Add the coconut milk, sugar and fish sauce, and cook over medium heat until the sauce begins to boil and thicken. Taste, and adjust the seasoning as needed with sugar and fish sauce. (If the sauce tastes a little bitter, add a bit more sugar.) Set aside to cool.

4. Rinse the fish under cold running water, and pat dry with paper towels. Season with lemon juice, salt and pepper.

5. Pour ⅓ of the cooled curry sauce over the fish fillets and marinate, refrigerated, for at least 30 minutes but no longer than four hours.

6. Lightly oil the banana leaves, then wrap each fillet in an oiled leaf to make a little parcel; cover each parcel with aluminum foil. Grill over medium-high heat until the fish is just cooked through, about 3 to 4 minutes per side. (Or, you may roast the fish in a 400 degree F oven until just cooked through, about 8 to 10 minutes.)

7. Reheat the remaining curry sauce over medium heat until warmed throughout. If needed, add a little bit of warm water to thin.

8. Unwrap the parcels, discard the foil and serve the fish fillets on the banana leaves with a generous amount of sauce spooned over each fillet. Garnish with cilantro leaves, and serve with steamed jasmine rice.

*Available at your local Asian market

Mrs. Sally's Sambal–Wrapped Fish
Serves 6

6 (8-ounce)	flaky white fish fillets (such as snapper or striped bass)
	salt and pepper, to taste
2 tablespoons	ground turmeric
2 tablespoons	Knorr® Tamarind Soup Base*
6 medium	banana leaves,* fresh or frozen, trimmed to fit size of fillets
¾ cup	Sambal (see recipe on page 111)
	Steamed Jasmine Rice (see recipe on page 144), as an accompaniment

Special Equipment: toothpicks, as needed

1. Rinse the fish under cold running water, and pat dry with paper towel. Season both sides of each fillet generously with salt, pepper, turmeric and tamarind soup base.

2. Lightly oil the banana leaves. Place one seasoned fillet in the middle of an oiled banana leaf, and spread 2 tablespoons of Sambal over the top. Wrap the fish in the leaf to make a little parcel, and secure the parcel with toothpicks. Continue making parcels in the same manner with the remaining ingredients.

3. Grill over medium-high heat until the fish is just cooked through, about 3 to 4 minutes per side. (Or, if you prefer, you may roast the fish in a 400 degree F oven until just cooked through, about 8 to 10 minutes.)

4. Unwrap the parcels, and serve the fish fillets on the banana leaves along with steamed jasmine rice.

Available at your local Asian market.

Louie's Note: Mrs. Sally owns a little Asian market right here in Ridgeland, Mississippi called Van Hung. Every time I shop there, she has something good to eat for her family - but she loves to offer me some. Of course, I don't turn it down. She is a great chef! This recipe was given to me by Mrs. Sally. It's a fun meal and makes a great presentation. You will feel like a real chef!

Sides

Lemon Roasted Edamame
Serves 2 to 4

1 (16-ounce) bag	frozen unshelled edamame* (Japanese green soybeans)
1 tablespoon	extra-virgin olive oil
2 tablespoons	fresh lemon juice
2 teaspoons	lemon zest
½ teaspoon	cayenne pepper, or to taste
½ teaspoon	kosher salt, or to taste

1. Preheat the oven to 400 degrees F. Cook the edamame in boiling salted water until almost tender, about 3 minutes. Immediately plunge into a bowl of ice water, then drain well; pat completely dry with paper towels.

2. Place the edamame in a large mixing bowl; add the oil, lemon juice, lemon zest, cayenne and salt, and toss to combine.

3. Arrange the beans on a baking sheet in a singer layer. Place in the oven and roast, uncovered, until the beans are just beginning to turn light golden brown, about 10 minutes.

4. Remove the beans from the oven; transfer to a serving dish and serve hot, cold or at room temperature.

Available at your local Asian market.

Broccoli and Garlic

Serves 4

1 pound	fresh broccoli florets (about 1 head)
3 tablespoons	extra-virgin olive oil
2 tablespoons	minced garlic
½ teaspoon	crushed red pepper flakes, or to taste
	salt and pepper, to taste

1. Cook the broccoli in rapidly boiling salted water for 1 minute; quickly drain, then plunge into a bowl of ice water to stop the cooking. Immediately drain the cooled broccoli, and pat completely dry with paper towel.

2. Heat a large sauté pan over medium-high heat; add the oil and heat through. Add the garlic and crushed red pepper flakes, and sauté for about 30 seconds. Before the garlic begins to brown, add the broccoli to the pan. Cook, stirring often, until tender, about 3 to 4 minutes. Season with salt and pepper, and serve warm or at room temperature.

Sesame Asparagus
Serves 4

Dressing:

1 tablespoon	soy sauce (or low-sodium soy sauce), or to taste
2 teaspoons	finely minced fresh ginger
1 teaspoon	lemon zest
1 tablespoon	fresh lemon juice
⅛ teaspoon	crushed red pepper flakes, or to taste
2 tablespoons	toasted sesame oil

Asparagus:

24 stalks	fresh asparagus (1 to 2 pounds), trimmed
1½ teaspoons	toasted white sesame seeds, for garnish
1½ teaspoons	toasted black sesame seeds, for garnish

For the Dressing:

1. In a small bowl, whisk together the soy sauce, ginger, lemon zest, lemon juice, crushed red pepper flakes and sesame oil. Taste and adjust the seasoning with soy sauce and crushed red pepper flakes.

For the Asparagus:

2. Cook the asparagus in boiling salted water until tender but still crisp, about 5 minutes. Do not over-cook, or the asparagus will lose its vibrant color!

3. Drain the asparagus, then plunge into a large bowl filled with ice water; quickly drain in a colander, then pat dry with paper towels; set aside.

4. To serve, arrange the asparagus spears on a serving platter. Drizzle the dressing over the asparagus, then sprinkle with the toasted sesame seeds. Serve at room temperature.

Roasted Sweet Potato Fries

Serves 6

	vegetable oil cooking spray, as needed
2 pounds	sweet potatoes, peeled and cut into fries
¼ cup	extra-virgin olive oil
2 tablespoons	Bruno's Dry Adobo Seasoning
	(or Creole seasoning), or to taste

1. Preheat the oven to 450 degrees F. Spray a large baking sheet with vegetable oil cooking spray. (You may need more than one baking sheet.)

2. In a large bowl, toss the sweet potatoes with the olive oil and adobo. Spread the seasoned fries on a baking sheet in a single even layer. Roast until golden brown and crispy, about 20 to 30 minutes. Turn about halfway through cooking time. Serve hot.

Louie's Note: You must make sure you turn the fries halfway through cooking. So, about 15 minutes after you have placed them in the oven, give them a good turn with a metal spatula. They will crisp up like a charm!

Grilled Vegetables
Serves 4

Marinade:

¼ cup	fresh lemon juice (about 2 lemons)
2 cloves	garlic, minced
2 tablespoons	dried Italian herbs
½ cup	extra-virgin olive oil
1 tablespoon	Bruno's Dry Adobo Seasoning (or Creole seasoning), or to taste

Vegetables:

1 medium	yellow squash, sliced into ½-inch thick rounds on the bias
1 large	red bell pepper, stem, seeds and ribs removed, quartered
1 medium	zucchini, sliced into ½-inch thick rounds on the bias
2 large	portobello mushrooms, gills removed (see Louie's Note) salt and pepper, to taste
3 tablespoons	finely chopped fresh parsley leaves, for garnish
3 tablespoons	grated Parmesan cheese, for garnish

For the Marinade:

1. In a large mixing bowl, whisk together the lemon juice, garlic, herbs, oil and adobo; set aside.

For the Vegetables:

2. Toss the vegetables in the marinade; set aside.

3. Preheat the grill to medium-high; clean and oil the grates to prevent sticking. Season the vegetables with salt and pepper, then grill until lightly charred on the outside and tender on the inside, about 4 to 5 minutes per side. When cool enough to handle, slice the portobellos and bell pepper into thick strips.

4. Arrange the grilled vegetables on a platter, and garnish with chopped parsley and Parmesan cheese. Serve warm or at room temperature.

Louie's Note: To remove the gills on a portobello, just pull off the stem then scrape out the brown stuff with a spoon. It only takes a few seconds, and it gives the mushroom a much nicer texture.

Thai Fried Rice

Serves 4

3 tablespoons	canola oil
1 medium	yellow onion, finely diced
2 large	eggs, beaten
2 cups	cooked and chilled brown rice
	(pre-cooked microwavable bag rice is fine)
3 tablespoons	Maggi® Seasoning,* or to taste
3 tablespoons	fresh lime juice (about 2 limes)
	salt and pepper, to taste
2 to 3 each	green onions, green parts only, thinly sliced
¼ cup	fresh cilantro leaves
½ cup	cooked and shelled edamame beans*
	(Japanese green soybeans)
	lime wedges, for garnish
	Asian chile powder,* for garnish (optional)

1. Heat a large wok or a non-stick sauté pan over high heat; add the oil and heat through.

2. Add the onion and cook, tossing and stirring constantly (stir-frying), for about 1 minute. Add the eggs, and stir-fry them too.

3. Add the rice, and toss to combine with the other ingredients. Stir in the Maggi and lime juice. Taste it, and see what else it needs to balance the flavors. Add salt and pepper to suit your taste.

4. Remove the fried rice from the heat; add the green onions, cilantro and edamame, and toss to combine.

5. Divide the fried rice between 4 dinner plates; garnish with lime wedges and chile powder. Encourage your guests to flavor their individual portion to their own taste with a squeeze of lime or an extra pinch of Asian chile powder. Serve hot.

Available at your local Asian market.

Louie's Note: You can add some cooked shrimp, chicken, crab or tofu to this dish, and you will love it even more!

Spanish White Rice

Serves 8

2 tablespoons	extra-virgin olive oil
2 strips	bacon (or turkey bacon), cut into 1-inch pieces
1 teaspoon	minced garlic
2 each	bay leaves
3 cups	long-grain white rice
6 cups	water
1 teaspoon	kosher salt, or to taste
¼ teaspoon	freshly ground black pepper, or to taste

1. Heat a medium saucepan over medium heat; add the oil and heat through. Add the bacon and cook until the fat has rendered and the bacon is crisp, about 3 minutes. Add the garlic and bay leaves, and cook until fragrant, about 1 minute more.

2. Add the rice and sauté for about 1 minute, making sure the rice is well coated with oil. Add the water, salt and pepper, and stir well.

3. Decrease the heat and simmer, uncovered, until the water has evaporated, about 20 to 30 minutes. Turn off the heat, cover and let set until the rice is tender, about 15 minutes more. Serve hot.

Steamed Jasmine Rice

Makes 4 cups

2 cups	jasmine rice
2 (1-inch) pieces	fresh ginger, peeled
2¼ cups	cool water

1. Rinse the rice under cold running water. Drain, then place the rice and ginger in a medium saucepan.

2. Add the 2¼ cups water and bring to a rolling boil over high heat. Cover, reduce the heat to low, and simmer for 20 minutes without stirring (or peeking).

3. Remove the pan from the heat, leaving the lid secured. Wait 10 minutes, then fluff the rice with a fork. Serve hot.

> **Louie's Note:** Use a rice cooker, and it will come out perfectly every time.

Arroz con Gandules

Serves 8 to 10

1 tablespoon	extra-virgin olive oil
3 slices	bacon (or turkey bacon), diced
½ cup	diced yellow onions
2 cloves	garlic, minced
1 (15-ounce) can	pigeon peas (gandules)* or black-eyed peas
1 packet	Goya® Sazon with Coriander and Annatto*
½ cup	tomato sauce
4 cups	water
	salt and pepper, to taste
2 cups	long-grain white rice (or brown rice)

1. Place a large, deep sauté pan over medium heat; add the oil and heat through. Add the bacon and cook until the fat has rendered and the bacon is crip, about 3 to 4 minutes.

2. Add the onions and cook until tender, about 5 minutes. Add the garlic and cook until fragrant, about 1 minute more.

3. Stir in all of the remaining ingredients except the rice. Season with salt and pepper if desired. Bring to a boil.

4. Stir in the rice, then cover and reduce the heat to a simmer. Simmer until the rice is tender, about 35 to 40 minutes. Serve hot.

Available in the Spanish section of most grocery stores or in your local Spanish market.

Mixed Vegetable Curry
Serves 6

¼ cup	canola oil
¼ cup	Sambal (see recipe on page 111)
3 tablespoons	curry powder
1 pound	fresh carrots, cut into very thin rounds at a diagonal
2 medium	Japanese eggplants, cut into ¼-inch thick rounds (or 1 small globe eggplant, cut into ½-inch pieces)
2 cups	string beans, trimmed and cut into 1½-inch pieces
3 cups	chicken or vegetable broth
1 (13.5-ounce) can	unsweetened coconut milk* (or light coconut milk)
3 cups	Chinese cabbage (or your favorite cabbage)
1 tablespoon	granulated sugar (or Splenda®)
1 teaspoon each	kosher salt and freshly ground black pepper, or to taste
	Steamed Jasmine Rice (see recipe on page 144), as an accompaniment

1. Heat a wok or 2 to 3-quart saucepan over medium heat; add the oil and heat through. Add the Sambal and curry powder, and cook, stirring and tossing constantly (stir-frying) for about 3 minutes.

2. Add the carrots, eggplant and string beans to the Sambal mixture and stir-fry until beginning to soften, about 5 to 10 minutes more.

3. Add the chicken broth, thin coconut milk,* cabbage, sugar, salt and pepper, and simmer until the vegetables are all tender.

4. Remove the curry from the heat, and stir in the reserved thick coconut cream from the top of the can. Taste, and adjust the seasoning as needed with salt and pepper. Serve hot with steamed jasmine rice.

Do not shake the can of coconut milk. Remove and reserve the thick cream from the top of the can – you will add it in at the end of the cooking time. Cook only with the thin coconut milk.

Louie's Note: Also great served over Asian noodles - or just by itself!

Asian Coleslaw

Serves 8

½ cup	unseasoned rice vinegar
	zest and juice of 2 oranges
	zest and juice of 2 limes
2 teaspoons	Bruno's Citrus Herb Seasoning
	(or your favorite citrus seasoning), or to taste
½ teaspoon	kosher salt, or to taste
1 teaspoon	granulated sugar (or Splenda®), or to taste
2 (16-ounce) bags	coleslaw mix
1 small	red onion, cut into thin strips
1 small bunch	green onions, green tops only, very thinly sliced
1 small	red bell pepper, stem, seeds and ribs removed, cut into thin strips
1 cup	fresh cilantro leaves

1. In a large bowl, whisk together the rice vinegar, orange zest and juice, lime zest and juice, citrus herb seasoning, salt and sugar.

2. Add the coleslaw mix, red onions, green onions, red bell peppers and cilantro to the bowl, and toss to mix well. Taste, and adjust the seasoning as needed with citrus herb seasoning, salt and sugar. Refrigerate for at least one hour before serving. (Serve with a slotted spoon.)

Mushrooms Sautéed in Spanish Sherry

Serves 4

6 tablespoons	extra-virgin olive oil
1½ pounds	small cremini mushrooms (or button mushrooms)
1 teaspoon	kosher salt, or to taste
¼ teaspoon	freshly ground black pepper, or to taste
1 small	yellow onion, finely diced
1 tablespoon	minced garlic
½ cup	good quality dry Spanish sherry
¼ cup	fresh parsley, chopped

1. Heat a large sauté pan over medium-high heat; add the oil and heat through.

2. Add the mushrooms, salt and pepper, and cook until the mushrooms stop producing liquid, about 10 to 15 minutes.

3. Add the onions and cook until tender, about 5 minutes; add the garlic and cook 1 minute more.

4. Add the sherry, and simmer until the liquid has evaporated, about 5 to 10 minutes. Taste, and adjust the seasoning as needed with salt and pepper.

5. Garnish with fresh parsley, and serve hot or at room temperature.

Louie's Note: Great little starter with some fresh baked bread.

Asian Snow Peas

Serves 4

2 cups	snow peas
¼ cup	soy sauce (or low-sodium soy sauce)
1 teaspoon	crushed red pepper flakes, or to taste
2 teaspoons	finely minced fresh ginger
1 tablespoon	canola oil

1. Carefully remove all the stems and strings from the snow peas.

2. In a small bowl, stir together the soy sauce, red pepper flakes and ginger; set aside.

3. Heat a small wok or sauté pan to high heat; add the oil and heat through. When the oil is very hot, add the peas, tossing and stirring constantly (stir-frying) until the peas are bright green, about 3 to 5 minutes. (Note: If the peas become yellow-green, that means you just over-cooked them!)

4. Add the soy mixture to the peas, and stir-fry 1 minute more. Serve immediately.

Louie's Note: These peas go great with any kind of grilled fish with just a little squeeze of lemon juice.

Cauliflower Mash
Serves 6

2 heads	fresh cauliflower florets
1½ quarts	chicken broth (6 cups)
½ cup	instant mashed potatoes
	salt and pepper, to taste

1. Combine the cauliflower and chicken broth in a medium saucepan over high heat; bring to a boil. Immediately reduce the heat and simmer until the cauliflower is tender, about 10 to 15 minutes.

2. Drain the cauliflower, leaving about ¼ cup of the broth in the saucepan.

3. Return the cooked cauliflower to the saucepan, and add the instant mashed potatoes. With a hand held blender (or food processor) blend to a mashed potato consistency. Season with salt and pepper to taste. Serve hot.

Cauliflower with Caper Vinaigrette
Serves 4

1 head	cauliflower florets
2 tablespoons	small capers
1 teaspoon	minced garlic
1 small	shallot, minced
1 teaspoon	crushed red pepper flakes, or to taste
¼ teaspoon each	kosher salt and freshly ground black pepper, or to taste
2 tablespoons	Spanish sherry vinegar (or balsamic vinegar)
¼ cup	extra-virgin olive oil

1. Bring a medium saucepan of salted water to a boil; cook the cauliflower until tender yet still crisp, about 5 minutes. Drain well, then pat dry with paper towels.

2. Combine the capers, garlic, shallots, crushed red pepper flakes, salt, pepper and vinegar in a blender; pulse to combine. With the motor running, slowly drizzle in the olive oil until creamy and emulsified. Taste, and season with salt and pepper.

3. Toss the cauliflower with the vinaigrette, and serve at room temperature.

Desserts

Kahlúa Chocolate Fudge Brownies

Serves 16

	butter-flavored vegetable oil cooking spray, as needed
2 cups	unsalted butter (or healthy butter alternative such as Smart Balance® Buttery Spread), brought to room temperature
1½ cups	light brown sugar (or Splenda® brown sugar)
1½ cups	granulated sugar (or Splenda®)
6 cups	semisweet chocolate chips
8 large	eggs, beaten
2 tablespoons	Kahlúa® coffee liqueur
2 cups	all-purpose flour (or whole-wheat flour)
2 teaspoons	kosher salt

1. Preheat the oven to 350 degrees F. Line a 9 x 13-inch glass baking dish with aluminum foil leaving some foil hanging over both ends. Spray the aluminum foil with butter-flavored vegetable oil cooking spray.

2. Combine the butter, brown sugar and granulated sugar in a medium saucepan over medium heat; cook, stirring constantly, until the mixture is smooth. Add the chocolate to the butter mixture and cook, stirring constantly, until the chocolate is melted and smooth. Do not over-cook!

3. Place the chocolate mixture in an electric mixer with the paddle attachment. Add the eggs, and mix for about 3 minutes on medium speed. Scrape down the sides and bottom of the bowl with a rubber spatula, then add the Kahlúa, flour and salt. Mix well for 2 minutes, then scrape down the bowl a final time and mix 3 minutes more.

4. Pour the batter into a baking dish, and smooth the top of the batter with a rubber spatula. Bake in the preheated oven until a toothpick inserted into the center of the brownies comes out slightly moist, about 1 hour. (Do not over-bake – the brownies should be gooey.) Allow the brownies to cool for 2 hours before serving.

Louie's Note: Don't be alarmed if the brownies start to crack while they are baking - that's actually a good thing! They are just doing what they are supposed to do.

Flan

(Caramel Custard)

Serves 8

1 (14-ounce) can	condensed milk
1 (12-ounce) can	evaporated milk
3 large	whole eggs
5 large	egg yolks
2 tablespoons	rum extract
2 cups	granulated sugar

1. Preheat the oven to 375 degrees F. Combine the condensed milk, evaporated milk, eggs, egg yolks and rum extract in a blender; mix well. Skim off any foam that forms on the top, and discard. Set the custard aside until needed.

2. To make the caramel, cook the sugar in a small saucepan over medium heat, stirring occasionally, until the sugar is a light amber color, about 15 to 20 minutes.

3. Wearing oven mitts to protect your hands and arms, carefully pour the caramel into the bottom of an 8-inch cake pan. (Exercise extreme caution, as the boiling hot sugar can inflict very serious burns!) Tilt the pan and swirl the caramel to coat the sides of the pan as well. Work quickly, as the caramel will harden within a matter of seconds.

4. Pour the custard mixture on top of the hardened caramel. Place the cake pan of flan in a roasting pan, and place in the oven; add just enough simmering water to come halfway up the sides of the cake pan. This is called baking in a water bath. (Be very careful to avoid getting water in the flan!)

5. Bake, uncovered, for 15 minutes. Reduce the heat to 350 degrees F and continue to bake until set, about 40 to 45 minutes. (If the flan is starting to brown, cover loosely with a sheet of oiled aluminum foil.) Remove from the oven, and transfer to a wire rack to cool. When cool to the touch, place in the refrigerator to chill thoroughly.

6. To serve, run a knife around the inside edge of the pan, and invert the flan onto a serving platter. (See Louie's Note.) Slice into wedges, and serve immediately.

Tembleque
(Coconut Pudding)
Serves 6

1 medium	vanilla bean
1 (15-ounce) can	cream of coconut* (such as Coco Lopez®)
2 cups	whole milk (or 2% milk)
¼ cup	granulated sugar (or Splenda®)
1 teaspoon	vanilla extract
½ cup	cornstarch
	ground cinnamon, for garnish

1. Split the vanilla bean in half lengthwise; use a paring knife to scrape out the seeds.

2. In a medium saucepan, whisk together the cream of coconut, milk, sugar, vanilla extract and vanilla bean seeds.

3. In a medium bowl, whisk together the cornstarch and ½ cup of the coconut mixture until the cornstarch has completely dissolved.

4. Whisk the cornstarch mixture into the saucepan with the coconut mixture. Cook over medium-high heat, stirring constantly, until the mixture begins to boil. Lower the heat to medium, and simmer until the sauce thickens, about 1 to 2 minutes more.

5. Working quickly, ladle the mixture into 6 individual ramekins (or 1 large flan mold). Cool to room temperature, then refrigerate for at least 2 hours and up to overnight.

6. To serve, unmold the puddings, and sprinkle with cinnamon. Serve cold.

If the coconut cream is too thick, microwave it until you achieve the desired consistency, about 30 to 45 seconds depending upon your microwave.

Louie's Note: If your Flan or Tembleque gets stuck in the pan, simply dip the bottom of the pan into hot water. Run a small knife around the inside edge of the pan, and your custard should slide right out.

White Chocolate Banana Tart with Rum Caramel Sauce
Makes 1 (10-inch) tart

Crust:

2 cups	vanilla wafer crumbs (or sugar-free vanilla wafer crumbs)
½ cup	ground macadamia nuts (2 ounces)
1 stick	lightly salted butter (or healthy butter alternative such as Smart Balance® Buttery Spread), melted (½ cup)

Tart:

2 tablespoons	all-purpose flour (or oat flour)
¾ cup	granulated sugar (or Splenda®)
6 large	egg yolks
2 cups	whole milk (or 2% milk)
2 teaspoons	vanilla extract
4 ounces	white chocolate, finely chopped (about ½ cup)
2 to 3 medium	bananas, peeled and sliced into rounds

Meringue:

6 large	egg whites, brought to room temperature
½ teaspoon	cream of tartar
1½ cups	granulated sugar (or Splenda®)
	mint sprigs, for garnish
	Rum Caramel Sauce (see recipe on page 175), as an accompaniment

Special Equipment: 10-inch removable-bottom tart pan

For the Crust:

1. Preheat the oven to 350 degrees F. Lightly spray a 10-inch removable-bottom tart pan with cooking spray. Mix together the vanilla wafer crumbs, ground macadamia nuts and melted butter in a medium bowl. Press the crumb mixture into the bottom of the pan and slightly up the sides. Bake until golden brown, about 5 minutes; set aside to cool.

For the Tart:

2. In a medium bowl, whisk together the flour and sugar; add the egg yolks and whisk to combine.

3. Bring the milk to a boil in a medium saucepan over medium-high heat. Temper the eggs by whisking half of the hot milk into the egg mixture; then pour the tempered egg mixture back into the saucepan. Whisk like crazy while the mixture comes to a boil; cook until the custard is thick and pulling away from the sides of the pan, about 3 minutes. Remove from the heat.

4. Whisk in the vanilla and white chocolate until the custard is completely smooth. Using a rubber spatula, push the custard through a coarse sieve into a clean bowl; place a sheet of plastic wrap directly onto the surface of the custard. Place in an ice water bath to cool quickly.

5. Fill the cooled tart shell with the cooled filling, then press a layer of sliced bananas into the filling. Place in the refrigerator to chill until set, at least 2 hours and up to 2 days.

For the Meringue:

6. Beat the egg whites and cream of tartar in an electric mixer with the whisk attachment until soft peaks begin to form. Slowly add the sugar, beating until the sugar dissolves and medium peaks form. (Do not over-mix or the meringue will be dry and lumpy!)

7. Spread the meringue evenly over the top of the custard and all the way to the edges; use a spoon to create soft peaks. For best results, use a culinary blow torch to brown the meringue. (Alternatively, bake at 350 degrees F until lightly browned, about 10 minutes. Transfer to a wire rack to cool to room temperature before placing back in the refrigerator to chill completely before serving.)

8. To serve, slice the tart into wedges; garnish each wedge with a mint sprig, and serve chilled on a pool of Rum Caramel Sauce.

Louie's Note: This dessert KICKS some serious you know what! It was always a best-seller at my restaurant.

Helado de Café

(Coffee Ice Cream)

Makes 7 cups

1¼ cups	granulated sugar (or Splenda®)
12 large	egg yolks
4 cups	heavy cream (or 2 cups half-and-half plus 2 cups 2% milk)
¼ cup	Kahlúa® coffee liqueur
½ cup	strong brewed coffee

1. In a medium mixing bowl, whisk together the sugar and egg yolks until pale yellow in color.

2. Combine the cream, Kahlúa and coffee in a small saucepan over medium heat; bring to a boil, then immediately reduce to a simmer.

3. Whisk a small amount of the hot coffee cream into the egg mixture to temper; pour the tempered egg mixture back into the saucepan, and place back on medium heat.

4. Cook, stirring constantly, until the mixture coats the back of a spoon.

5. Remove the pan from the heat, and strain through a coarse sieve into a glass or stainless steel bowl. Place in an ice water bath to cool quickly, then place in the refrigerator to chill overnight.

6. Freeze the ice cream according to the manufacturer's instructions. Store, tightly covered, in the freezer for up to one month.

Louie's Apple Crisp with Raisins
Serves 4

	butter-flavored vegetable oil cooking spray, as needed
3 medium	Granny Smith apples, peeled, cored and thinly sliced
1 teaspoon	ground cinnamon
1 pinch	nutmeg
1 tablespoon	granulated sugar (or Splenda®)
2 tablespoons	raisins
3 tablespoons	water
1 cup	nonfat vanilla yogurt
1 cup	low-fat granola
	fresh mint sprigs, for garnish

1. Lightly spray a medium non-stick sauté pan with butter-flavored cooking spray; place over medium heat. Add the apples, cinnamon, nutmeg, sugar and raisins, and cook for 3 minutes; add the water and cook until the apples are tender yet still firm, about 2 to 3 minutes more.

2. Transfer the apple mixture to a clean bowl; cool to room temperature, then place in the refrigerator for at least 30 minutes and up to overnight.

3. To assemble the crisp, divide the apple mixture amongst 4 small bowls; top each with ¼ cup yogurt and ¼ cup granola; garnish with fresh mint sprigs, and serve immediately.

Louie's Note: Add fresh or frozen berries for a colorful and tasty twist. This dessert is one that will help to control your hunger for chocolate cake or cheesecake!

Key Lime Cheesecake
with Chocolate Cookie Crust
Makes 1 (10-inch) cheesecake

	butter-flavored vegetable oil cooking spray, as needed
2½ cups	OREO® cookie crumbs (about 35 OREOs crushed)(or sugar-free chocolate cookie crumbs)
¼ cup	melted lightly salted butter (or melted healthy butter alternative such as Smart Balance® Buttery Spread)
1½ pounds	cream cheese (or low-fat cream cheese), brought to room temperature
2 tablespoons	all-purpose flour (or oat flour)
1⅛ cups	granulated sugar (or Splenda®)
4 large	eggs, beaten
¼ cup	whole milk (or 2% milk)
1 cup	fresh or bottled key lime juice
	whipped cream, for garnish (optional)
	lime wheels, for garnish (optional)

Special Equiptment: 1 (10-inch) springform pan

1. Preheat the oven to 300 degrees F. Lightly spray a 10-inch springform pan with cooking spray. Mix together the chocolate cookie crumbs and melted butter in a medium bowl. Press the crumb mixture into the bottom of the pan and slightly up the sides. Bake for 5 minutes, and set aside.

2. Beat the cream cheese in an electric mixer with the paddle attachment until smooth, about 3 minutes. (Before adding each ingredient, scrape down the sides and bottom of the bowl with a rubber spatula.)

3. Add the flour and sugar, and mix to combine. Add the eggs, one at a time, mixing to combine after each addition. Add the milk and key lime juice, and beat until smooth, about 3 minutes. Continue scraping the sides and bottom of the bowl as needed.

4. Pour the batter into the crust. Bake in the preheated oven until just set, about 1 hour and 15 minutes. Remove from the oven, and cool to room temperature on a rack.

5. Place in the refrigerator and chill for at least 8 hours before serving. Garnish with whipped cream and lime wheels, if desired.

Enchilada de Fruita

Serves 6

	butter flavored vegetable oil cooking spray
1 (20-ounce) can	apple pie filling (or sugar-free apple pie filling)
1½ cups	mixed fresh or frozen berries
1 teaspoon	ground cinnamon, plus extra as needed
2 teaspoons	vanilla extract
6 (8-inch)	flour tortillas (or whole-wheat tortillas)
⅓ cup	lightly salted butter (or healthy butter alternative such as Smart Balance® Buttery Spread)
½ cup	granulated sugar (or Splenda®)
½ cup	brown sugar (or Splenda® brown sugar)
½ cup	water
	confectioners' sugar, for garnish (optional)

1. Preheat the oven to 350 degrees F. Spray a 9 x 13-inch baking dish with vegetable oil cooking spray. In a medium bowl, mix together the apple pie filling, berries, cinnamon and vanilla.

2. Place a tortilla on a clean work surface; put 1/6 of the fruit mixture on the lower part of your tortilla, and gently roll into an enchilada. Continue with the remaining tortillas and fruit mixture. Place the enchiladas seam-side down in the oiled baking dish, and set aside.

3. Combine the butter, sugar, brown sugar and water in a medium saucepan over medium-high heat; bring to a boil. Immediately reduce the heat and simmer, stirring constantly, for about 3 to 5 minutes.

4. Pour the sauce evenly over the enchiladas, and sprinkle with cinnamon (if desired). Bake in the preheated oven until warmed through, about 30 minutes. Sprinkle with confectioners' sugar (if desired) and serve hot.

Louie's Note: Use the substitute ingredients like sugar-free pie filling and Splenda®, and this is a great low-calorie dessert. Enjoy it without feeling guilty – and if you really want to be naughty – add a scoop of reduced fat sugar-free frozen yogurt. Garnish with additional fresh berries for a beautiful presentation.

Tres Leches

(Three Milks Cake)

Serves 10 to 15

Cake:

2¼ cups	all-purpose flour
½ teaspoon	kosher salt
1⅛ teaspoons	baking powder
¾ cup	unsalted butter
3 cups	granulated sugar
8 large	eggs
2¼ teaspoons	vanilla extract

Milks:

1 (14-ounce) can	condensed milk
1 (5-ounce) can	evaporated milk
1 cup	heavy cream
2 tablespoons	rum extract

Icing:

2 cups	heavy cream, chilled
2 tablespoons	vanilla extract
2 tablespoons	light corn syrup
½ cup	confectioners' sugar

For the Cake:

1. Preheat the oven to 350 degrees F. Grease a 9 x 13-inch baking pan, and line the bottom with parchment paper.

2. Sift together the flour, salt and baking powder; set aside.

3. In an electric mixer with the paddle attachment, beat the butter and sugar on medium speed until fluffy, about 3 minutes; this is called creaming. Add the eggs and vanilla, and beat well to combine.

4. Add the flour mixture to the butter mixture in 3 stages, mixing to combine after each addition. Scrape down the sides and bottom of the bowl with a rubber spatula from time to time to avoid lumps in the batter. Pour the cake batter into the prepared pan and bake until the top of the cake springs back when lightly touched or a cake tester inserted into the center comes out clean, about 30 to 35 minutes. Set the cake aside to cool.

For the Milks:

5. While the cake is cooling down, whisk together the condensed milk, evaporated milk, cream and rum extract in a medium bowl.

6. Invert the cake onto a deep rectangular serving platter. Prick the cake with a fork multiple times all over the top, then slowly ladle the milk mixture over the cake, allowing it to soak in before adding more. Set aside.

For the Icing:

7. Combine the cream, vanilla, corn syrup and confectioners' sugar in an electric mixer with the whisk attachment; beat until the cream thickens enough to hold stiff peaks.

8. Spread a thick layer all over the cake, then place in the refrigerator to set for at least 1 to 2 hours before serving. Serve chilled.

Chocolate Chip Bread Pudding with Frangelico Sauce

Serves 8

	butter flavored vegetable oil cooking spray
1 (12-ounce) loaf	French bread (or whole-wheat French bread)
2 cups	whole milk (or 2% milk)
¾ cup	granulated sugar (or Splenda®)
1 large	whole egg
3 large	egg yolks
2 teaspoons	vanilla extract
½ cup	dark chocolate chips
⅓ cup	chopped pralines (optional) (purchase at any candy store)

Sauce:

1 cup	brown sugar (or Splenda® brown sugar)
½ cup	Frangelico® hazelnut liqueur

For the Pudding:

1. Preheat the oven to 350 degrees F. Spray an 8 x 8-inch baking dish with vegetable oil cooking spray; set aside. Cut the bread into manageable size pieces, and place in a food processor; pulse in batches to make small pieces. Place in a large bowl and set aside.

2. Combine the milk, sugar, egg, egg yolks and vanilla in a medium saucepan over low heat; whisk to combine. Simmer, stirring constantly with a silicone spatula, until the custard thickens slightly, about 3 to 5 minutes.

3. Pour the hot custard over the bread, and toss gently to mix. Set aside to cool completely. When cool, add the chocolate chips and pralines (if using), and toss gently to mix. Pour the pudding into the oiled baking dish, and bake until light golden brown and set, about 45 to 50 minutes.

For the Sauce:

4. While the pudding is baking, whisk together the brown sugar and Frangelico in a small saucepan over medium-high heat. Cook, stirring frequently, until the sugar has dissolved and the sauce is smooth.

5. Remove the bread pudding from the oven, and allow to set for 5 minutes before serving. Serve hot with Frangelico Sauce.

Lemon Curd Trifle with Fresh Berries

Serves 6

1 pint	fresh strawberries, hulled and sliced
1 pint	fresh blueberries
1 pint	fresh blackberries
1 loaf	lemon pound cake (or low-fat sugar-free pound cake), cut into bite-size cubes
2 cups	lemon curd (recipe folows) (or sugar-free lemon curd)
3 cups	sweetened whipped cream (or Cool Whip® Sugar-Free Whipped Topping)

1. Toss the berries together, and set aside.

2. Place a layer of pound cake cubes in the bottom of a glass trifle bowl. Spoon a layer of lemon curd over the pound cake, then top with a layer of berries and a layer of whipped cream.

3. Repeat making layers until all of the ingredients are used up. Chill well before serving.

Lemon Curd
Makes 3 cups

8 large	egg yolks
	zest of 3 lemons
½ cup	fresh lemon juice (about 6 lemons)
1 cup	granulated sugar (or Splenda®)
1 pinch	kosher salt
12 tablespoons	unsalted butter (or healthy butter alternative such as Smart Balance® Buttery Spread), cubed and brought to room temperature

1. Combine the eggs, zest, lemon juice, sugar and salt in a medium stainless-steel bowl; place over a pot of simmering water and whisk until the mixture has thickened, about 12 to 15 minutes. (If you have a double boiler, that will also work really well for this recipe.)

2. Add the butter cubes a few pieces at a time, stirring well after each addition.

3. Place the bowl of curd in a larger bowl filled with ice water, being very careful to prevent water from getting in the curd. The ice water bath will help the curd cool very quickly. Stir from time to time to help expedite the process.

4. The lemon curd is ready to eat once it reaches room temperature. If not using immediately store, tightly covered, in the refrigerator for up to 3 days.

Guilt-Free Bananas Foster
Serves 6

⅓ cup	healthy butter alternative
	(such as Smart Balance® Buttery Spread)
½ cup	Splenda® brown sugar
½ cup	Splenda®
½ cup	water
2 tablespoons	rum extract
2 tablespoons	banana extract
6 medium	bananas, quartered lengthwise
6 scoops	low-fat sugar-free vanilla frozen yogurt
	ground cinnamon, for garnish
½ cup	chopped toasted walnuts, for garnish (optional)

1. Combine the butter spread, Splenda brown sugar, Splenda, water, rum extract and banana extract in a large sauté pan over medium-high heat; bring to a boil. Immediately reduce the heat and simmer, stirring constantly, until the Splenda dissolves and the sauce thickens, about 3 to 5 minutes.

2. Stir in the bananas, and cook until soft and brown.

3. Place one scoop of frozen yogurt in each of 6 bowls. Top each with 4 pieces of banana and a generous spoonful of the warm Bananas Foster sauce. Sprinkle with cinnamon and toasted walnuts (if desired), and serve immediately.

Chocolate Macaroon Cookies
Makes 40 cookies

Macaroons:

3 large	egg whites
1 scant pinch	kosher salt
¾ cup	granulated sugar (or Splenda®)
5 cups	shredded sweetened coconut

Ganache:

½ cup	heavy whipping cream (or 2% milk)
¾ cup	semisweet or bittersweet chocolate chips
1 tablespoon	lightly salted butter (or healthy butter alternative such as Smart Balance® Buttery Spread)

For the Macaroons:

1. Preheat the oven to 350 degrees F. In a large bowl, stir together the egg whites, salt, sugar and coconut.

2. Scoop out the macaroons with a mini ice cream scoop; place onto a parchment paper-lined baking sheet, leaving a couple of inches between cookies. Lightly press on the top of each macaroon to slightly flatten.

3. Bake until light golden brown, about 15 to 20 minutes. Set aside to cool.

For the Ganache:

4. Heat the cream in a small saucepan over medium heat; bring to a simmer. Remove the pan from the heat, and add the chocolate chips and butter; stir until smooth. Refrigerate until thickened.

5. To assemble the macaroons, spread a ¼-inch thick layer of ganache on half of the macaroons. Top each with another macaroon to make a little chocolate sandwich. Lay the cookies on their sides until the ganache is firm. Serve with a cold glass of milk, and enjoy!

Louie's Note: A mini ice cream scoop holds about 2 teaspoons. Look for a #60 ice cream scoop – it should be the perfect size for making macaroons or scooping out sorbet to serve between courses.

Rum Caramel Sauce

Makes ½ cup

⅓ cup	lightly salted butter (or healthy butter alternative such as Smart Balance® Buttery Spread)
½ cup	granulated sugar (or Splenda®)
½ cup	dark brown sugar (or Splenda® brown sugar)
½ cup	water
2 tablespoons	dark rum (or rum extract)

Combine all of the ingredients in a medium saucepan over medium heat; simmer until the sauce has reduced by half, about 8 to 12 minutes. Serve warm.

Chocolate Sauce

Makes 1¼ cups

¼ cup	heavy cream (or 2% milk)
8 ounces	dark or semisweet chocolate chips
2 tablespoons	Kahlúa® coffee liqueur (or vanilla extract)

1. Simmer the heavy cream in a small saucepan over medium heat until it slightly bubbles around the edges.

2. Remove the pan from the heat; add the chocolate and Kahlúa, and stir until completely smooth. (If you need to hold warm for several hours, place in an insulated thermos.)

3. If not using within several hours, cool the sauce completely then store, tightly covered, in the refrigerator for up to 5 days. Reheat gently before serving.

Pasteles de Guayaba y Queso de Crema

(Guava and Cream Cheese Pastries)

Serves 6

8 ounces	cream cheese (or light cream cheese), brought to room temperature (1 cup)
8 ounces	lightly salted butter (or healthy butter alternative such as Smart Balance® Buttery Spread), brought to room temperature (1 cup)
2 cups	all-purpose flour
12 tablespoons	guava paste (or guava jelly)*

1. Combine the cream cheese, butter and flour in an electric mixer with the paddle attachment; beat just to combine. Do not over-mix, or the dough will be tough. Gather the dough into a ball, and wrap tightly with plastic wrap; refrigerate for 1 hour before rolling out.

2. Dust your work surface with flour to prevent sticking. Roll the dough out into a ¼-inch thick rectangle; cut out 12 equal size squares.

3. Place 1 tablespoonful of guava paste in the center of each dough square, and fold to form a triangle; press the edges to seal.

4. Arrange the pastries on a baking sheet, and bake until golden brown, about 25 to 30 minutes. Serve hot or at room temperature.

Available at your local Spanish market or online at www.tienda.com.

Louie's Note: I have fond memories of my grandfather sitting in front of the TV watching the Yankees play and enjoying a few of these with coffee...They are really delicious served with sliced manchego cheese!

Cabernet Poached Pears

Makes 5 pears

1 medium	vanilla bean, split lengthwise
2 each	bay leaves
1 to 2	whole cloves
5 to 6	cracked peppercorns
3 cups	dry red wine (about 1 standard bottle)
2 cups	water
3 pieces	orange zest (about 3-inches x ¼-inch)
1 cup	fresh orange juice (about 3 oranges)
1½ cups	granulated sugar (or Splenda®), or to taste
1 pinch	kosher salt
5 small	ripe but firm pears

1. Scrape the vanilla bean seeds into a large saucepot, then throw the bean into the pot. Make a little sachet or spice pouch with the bay leaves, cloves and cracked peppercorns. (Place in a square of cheesecloth and tie with butcher's twine.) Add the sachet to the pot.

2. Add the wine, water, orange zest and juice, sugar and salt; simmer over medium heat until highly aromatic, about 15 minutes; taste, and adjust the seasoning as needed with sugar.

3. Using a vegetable peeler, smoothly peel the pears from top to bottom, rotating around the pear. Cut the pears in half, and neatly scoop out the core and seeds with a melon baller.

4. Poach the pear halves (gently simmer at 160 to 180 degrees F) until almost tender, about 10 minutes. While poaching, place a heat-resistant plate slightly smaller than the circumference of the pot on top of the pears to keep them submerged. (Remember, the pears will continue to cook a bit more in the poaching liquid, even off the heat. When possible, allow the pears to soak in the poaching liquid for at least several hours - or up to 5 days.)

5. Remove the pears from the liquid, and serve chilled or at room temperature.

Louie's Note: If you are poaching the pears for the Pear, Blue Cheese and Vanilla Walnut Canapés (see recipe on page 28), you will only need 2 or 3 poached pears to make the canapés. But don't worry, the left-over pears are delicious served with ice cream and Vanilla Walnuts (see recipe on page 13).

Drinks

Coquitos

Serves 8

1 (13.5-ounce) can	unsweetened coconut milk, chilled
1 (15-ounce) can	cream of coconut*
	(such as Coco Lopez®), chilled
1 (12-ounce) can	evaporated milk, chilled
10 ounces	white rum (1¼ cups), chilled
3 ounces	brandy (about ⅓ cup)
1 tablespoon	vanilla extract
1 teaspoon	ground cinnamon, plus extra for garnish
	cinnamon sticks, for garnish

1. Combine all of the ingredients except the cinnamon sticks in a blender; process until frothy, about 2 minutes.

2. Transfer the mixture to a large glass pitcher, and refrigerate until ready to serve.

3. To serve, fill tall glasses with ice cubes, and pour the coquitos over the ice. Garnish with a sprinkle of cinnamon and a cinnamon stick, and serve immediately.

If the coconut cream is too thick, microwave it until you achieve the desired consistency, about 35 to 45 seconds depending upon your microwave.

Louie's Note: Traditionally, this celebratory holiday beverage is made with raw egg yolks, but I omitted the eggs for food safety purposes. Now everyone can enjoy it!

Christmas Cosmos with Poached Cranberries

Serves 4

Cranberries:

1 cup	water
2 cups	granulated sugar
2 strips	orange zest (3-inch x ¼-inch)
1 each	bay leaf
6 ounces	fresh cranberries (half 12-ounce bag)
5 to 6	fresh basil leaves

Cosmos:

8 ounces	vodka (1 cup)
8 ounces	cranberry juice (1 cup)
4 ounces	orange liqueur (such as Grand Marnier®)(½ cup)
	juice of 2 limes
	lime wheels, for garnish

Special Equipment: metal martini shaker; cocktail picks; martini glasses

For the Cranberries:

1. Combine the water, sugar, zest and bay leaf in a small saucepan over medium-high heat; bring to a boil. Reduce the heat and simmer, stirring occasionally, for 5 minutes; add the cranberries and continue simmering until the cranberries are tender, about 5 to 10 minutes. Do not over-cook, or the cranberries will burst.

2. Remove the pan from the heat, and stir in the basil leaves. Allow the cranberries to cool completely in the liquid; strain before using. (You may want to save the flavorful poaching liquid to sweeten other dishes!) Thread several poached cranberries onto each of 4 cocktail picks, and place in 4 martini glasses.

For the Cosmos:

3. Fill a metal martini shaker halfway with ice; shake for about 30 seconds.

4. Add the vodka, cranberry juice, orange liqueur and lime juice, and shake for another 10 to 15 seconds. Strain the cosmos into the glasses, and garnish with lime wheels; serve immediately.

Mango Martini
Serves 1

4 ounces	mango rum (½ cup)
1 ounce	Triple Sec (2 tablespoons)
1 ounce	mango puree (2 tablespoons)
1 ounce	margarita mix (2 tablespoons)
	juice of 1 lime

Special Equipment: martini shaker; chilled martini glass

1. Fill a metal martini shaker halfway with ice; shake for about 30 seconds.

2. Add the mango rum, Triple Sec, mango puree, margarita mix and lime juice, and shake for another 15 to 30 seconds.

3. Strain the martini into a chilled martini glass, and enjoy.

Lemon–Lime Mojito

Serves 1

8 to 10	fresh mint leaves, plus extra sprig for garnish
½ medium	lime, cut into wedges
½ medium	lemon, cut into wedges
2 tablespoons	mint simple syrup (see Louie's Note)
1½ ounces	citrus-flavored rum (such as Bacardi® Limón rum)
3 ounces	lemon-lime soda (such as Sprite® or 7-UP®)

<u>Special Equipment:</u> muddler

1. Using a muddler, gently crush the mint leaves, lime wedges and lemon wedges in a tall rocks glass.

2. Add the simple syrup, and fill the glass with ice.

3. Add the rum, then top off the mojito with soda; stir well to combine. Garnish with a sprig of mint, and serve immediately.

Louie's Note: To make mint-flavored simple syrup, boil equal parts of water and sugar in a medium saucepan over medium-high heat; cook until the sugar dissolves. Remove the pan from the heat, and add 1 small bunch of fresh mint; cool to room temperature. Strain the syrup, and place in the refrigerator to chill before using. Store in the refrigerator for up to 1 week.

Sangria
Serves 8

6 cups	red wine (about 2 standard bottles)
4 ounces	Triple Sec (or other orange liqueur) (½ cup)
4 ounces	brandy (½ cup)
1 (6-ounce) can	frozen orange juice concentrate, thawed
1 (6-ounce) can	frozen lemonade concentrate, thawed
¼ cup	granulated sugar (or Splenda®), or to taste
2 small	oranges, sliced into rounds, for garnish, divided
1 small	Granny Smith apple, cored and sliced into rounds, for garnish
½ cup	maraschino cherries, for garnish

1. In a large pitcher, mix together the wine, Triple Sec, brandy, orange juice concentrate, lemonade concentrate and sugar. Taste, and add additional sugar as desired. Chill well.

2. Before serving, add half of the orange rounds, apple rounds and cherries to the pitcher. Garnish each glass with an orange round, and serve immediately.

Louie's Note: Everyone loves this Sangria! It is quick and easy but just as delicious as any Sangria you'll ever taste. Serve it with your favorite tapas or Paella (see recipe on page 128).

Mango Margaritas
Makes about 1½ quarts

1 wedge	lime
½ cup	yellow or gold sanding or sparkling sugar
2 cups	chopped fresh mangos
	(or sliced fresh mangos in syrup), plus extra for garnish
2 cups	ice
1 cup	tequila
½ cup	Triple Sec
½ cup	fresh lime juice (about 6 limes)
½ cup	your favorite margarita mix

Special Equipment: 4 margarita glasses; cocktail picks

1. Moisten the rim of each chilled glass with the lime wedge; gently press each rim into the sugar. Skewer 2 or 3 pieces of mango on each cocktail pick, and drop one into each glass.

2. Combine the ice, diced mango, tequila, Triple Sec, lime juice and margarita mix in a blender; puree until smooth.

3. Pour the liquid into the prepared glasses, and serve immediately.

Razzmatazz Champagne
Serves 1

3 each	fresh raspberries, for garnish
4 ounces	chilled Champagne or sparkling wine (½ cup)
½ ounce	DeKuyper® Razzmatazz liqueur
	(or other raspberry liqueur) (1 tablespoon)

Special Equipment: Champagne flute; cocktail pick

1. Skewer 3 raspberries onto a cocktail pick; drop into the Champagne flute.

2. Pour the Champagne into the flute, then top off with the raspberry liqueur. Serve immediately.

Watermelon-Rum Punch

Serves 8

16 ounces	watermelon liqueur
	(such as DeKuyper® Watermelon Pucker-2 cups)
16 ounces	light rum (2 cups)
32 ounces	pineapple juice (4 cups)
8 ounces	sweet and sour mix (1 cup)
16 ounces	ginger ale (2 cups)
8 small	watermelon wedges, for garnish

1. In a large pitcher, mix together the watermelon liqueur, rum, pineapple juice, sweet and sour mix and ginger ale.

2. Fill 8 tall glasses with ice, then pour the watermelon-rum punch over the ice. Garnish each glass with a wedge of watermelon, and serve immediately.

Watermelon Agua Frescas
Serves 8

1 (10-pound)	ripe red seedless watermelon
2 cups	sparking mineral water, divided
½ cup	fresh lime juice (about 6 limes)
¾ cup	granulated sugar (or Splenda®), or to taste
¼ cup	fresh mint leaves, plus extra sprigs for garnish
2 cups	lemon-lime soda (such as Sprite® or 7-UP®) (or diet lemon-lime soda)

1. Cut the watermelon in half, then scoop out all of the juicy red flesh into a large bowl. Set aside.

2. Fill a blender about three-fourths of the way with watermelon; add ¼ cup sparkling water, and puree. Pour into a large glass pitcher. Continue with the remaining watermelon and sparkling water until all of the watermelon has been pureed. (If you run out of sparkling water before watermelon, just use some of the pureed watermelon juice to puree the remaining watermelon.)

3. Add the lime juice, sugar and mint leaves to the watermelon puree, and stir until the sugar has dissolved. Allow the mixture to set for one hour.

4. Add the soda to the pitcher, and stir well to combine. Fill 8 tall glasses with ice, then pour the watermelon agua frescas over the ice. Garnish each with a sprig of mint, and serve immediately.

Index

INDEX

Meat

Bistec Encebollado
Steak and Onions, 87

Chorizo, 61

Empanadas, 14, 15

Hoisin Lime Ribs, 97

Meatballs in Tomato Sauce, 93

Peppercorn-Crusted Filets
with Molasses-Rum Glaze, 94

Piononos,
Stuffed Sweet Plantain Rolls, 26, 27

Rellenos de Papa
Stuffed Potato Balls, 4, 5

Smoked BBQ Chipotle
Beef Tenderloin, 88

Smoked BBQ Chipotle Guava Ribs, 98

Thai Beef Lettuce Wraps, 25

Thai Spring Rolls with
Sweet and Sour Dipping Sauce, 22

Vaca Frita, Crispy Fried Beef, 90

Nuts

Crunchy Almonds
with Cayenne and Cumin, 12

Curry Cashews, 12

Pear, Blue Cheese
and Vanilla Walnut Canapés, 28

Vanilla Walnuts, 13

Olives

Marinated Olives, 8

Poultry

Asian Sesame Noodles
with Chicken and Broccoli, 62, 63

Bruno's Arroz con Pollo, 60

Chicken with Fresh Basil, 77

Chicken Satay, 2

Chiles Rellenos, Stuffed Chiles, 68, 69

Grilled Adobo Chicken
with Chimichurri, 64

Jerk Chicken with Mango Chutney, 72, 73

Papaya Honey Mustard
Baked Chicken, 66

Sambal Chicken, 65

Tea-Marinated Duck Breasts
with Apple Chutney, 78, 79

Thai Green Curry
with Chicken and Eggplant, 84

Salads

Asparagus Salad with
Roasted Red Peppers and Capers, 52

Crabby Louie, 48

Crispy Tomatoes with
Mozzarella and Fresh Thyme, 47

Cuban Salad, 50

Fresh Spinach Salad
with Salsa and Shredded Manchego, 51

Mieng Kum, 20

Thai Cucumber Salad, 3

Thai Grilled Eggplant Salad, 53

Roasted Corn Salsa, 55

Shrimp and Artichoke Salad, 46

Sauces

Apple Chutney, 79

Avocado Lime Crema, 102

Caribbean Mojo, 116

Chimichurri, 64

Chocolate Sauce, 175

Frangelico Sauce, 168

Fresh Cranberry-Pecan Relish, 89

Garlic and Cilantro Mojo, 35

Guilt-Free Chipolte BBQ Sauce, 99

Hoisin Peanut Sauce, 11

Honey Lemongrass Vinaigrette, 56

Lemon Curd, 171

Lemon Garlic Vinaigrette, 51

Mango Chutney, 73

Mieng Kum Sauce, 20, 21

Molasses-Rum Glaze, 94

Mole Negro, 70, 71

Papaya Honey Mustard, 66

Red Curry Sauce, 130

Roasted Garlic Vinaigrette, 57

Rosemary Butter, 125

Rum Caramel Sauce, 175

Sake-Soy-Tamarind Glaze, 108

Sambal, 111

Sofrito, 103

Spicy Basil Guacamole, 75

Sweet and Sour Dipping Sauce, 23

Thai Peanut Sauce, 3

Tropical Fruit Salsa, 116

Seafood

Bacalaitos, Fried Salt Cod Fritters, 36

Banana Leaf-Wrapped Fish
with Red Curry Sauce, 130, 131

Crab Fritters, 18, 19

Escabeche de Pescado,
Marinated Fish, 122

Grilled Bread with Smoked Salmon,
Manchego and Olives, 7

Macadamia Nut-Crusted Grouper,
with Tropical Fruit Salsa, 114

Miso-Marinated Sea Bass, 107

Mrs. Sally's Sambal-Wrapped Fish, 132

Paella, 128, 129

Salmon with Sake-Soy-Tamarind Glaze,
Grilled, 108, 109

Scallop Ceviche, 30

Sesame-Seared Tuna with
Edamame Hummus, 120, 121

Vietnamese Summer Rolls
with Fresh Crabmeat, 10, 11

Shrimp

Adobo Fried Shrimp Soft Tacos with
Smoked BBQ Chipotle Coleslaw, 117

Adobo-Rubbed Shrimp with Garlic
and Cilantro Mojo, Grilled, 34, 35

Garlic Shrimp, 123

Pad Thai with Shrimp, 118, 119

Rosemary-Garlic Shrimp, 124

Rosemary Shrimp Pasta, 112

Shrimp and Artichoke Salad, 46

Shrimp with Spicy Chili Sauce, 110

Spicy Bacon-Wrapped
Grilled Shrimp, 9

Spicy Mexican Shrimp Ceviche, 126

Sides

Arroz con Gandules, 145

Asian Coleslaw, 147

Asian Snow Peas, 151

BBQ Chipotle Coleslaw, 117

Soups

Sources

Sources

Asian Food Grocer
131 West Harris Avenue
South San Francisco, CA 94080
www.Asianfoodgrocer.com

*Batte Furniture
1010 East Northside Drive
Jackson, MS 39206
(601)-366-0335
www.battefurniture.com

*Bruno's Eclectic, Inc
P.O.Box 16785
Jackson, MS 39236
www.brunoseclectic.com

*Everyday Gourmet
1625 East County Line Road
Jackson, MS 39211
(601)-977-9258
www.theeverydaygourmet.com

Import Food
P.O.Box 2054
Issaquah, WA 98027
www.Importfood.com

Joe Lee Photography
4940 Terry Road
P.O. Box 7210-73
Byram, MS 39272
(601)-605-1945
www.joelee@joelee.com
joelee@joelee.com

La Tienda
3601 La Grange Parkway
Toano, VA 23168
www.Tienda.com

Lauren Farms
655 Napanee Road
Leland, MS 38756
1-662-686-2894
www.laurenfarms.com

Mid South Produce of Jackson
352 East Woodrow Wilson Ave.
Jackson, MS 39216
(601)-961-1452

Mr. Martinez
484 Bayamon Street
La Cumbre
San Juan, P.R. 00926
1-(407)-745-1448
www.elcolmadito.com

New Orleans Seafood
795 East McDowell Road
Jackson, MS 39204
(601)-969-0725

*Pearl River Glass Studio, Inc.
142 Millsaps Ave
Jackson, MS 39202
www.pearlriverglass.com

*Persnickety
2078 Main Street
Madison, MS 39110
(601)-853-9595

The Spanish Table
1426 Western Ave
Seattle, WA 98101
www.Spanishtable.com

Pick On Us, Inc.
P.O.Box 5417
Oceanside, CA 92052
www.Pickonus.com

Van Hung Asian Market
587 Highway 51 #P
Ridgeland, Ms 39157
(601)-856-9638

Swiss Chalet Fine Foods
7200 Wynn Park
Houston, TX 77008-6030
1-(713)-868-9505
www.scff.com

Bruno's Eclectic Glassware and Spices Available at * locations.